ROCHESTER

BY
CHARLES WILLIAMS

Copyright © 2018 Read Books Ltd.
This book is copyright and may not be
reproduced or copied in any way without
the express permission of the publisher in writing

British Library Cataloguing-in-Publication Data
A catalogue record for this book is available from
the British Library

CHARLES WILLIAMS

Charles Walter Stansby Williams was born in London in 1886. He dropped out of University College London in 1904, and was hired by Oxford University Press as a proof-reader, quickly rising to the position of editor. While there, arguably his greatest editorial achievement was the publication of the first major English-language edition of the works of the Danish philosopher Søren Kierkegaard.

Williams began writing in the twenties and went on to publish seven novels. Of these, the best-known are probably *War in Heaven* (1930), *Descent into Hell* (1937), and *All Hallows' Eve* (1945) – all fantasies set in the contemporary world. He also published a vast body of well-received scholarship, including a study of Dante entitled *The Figure of Beatrice* (1944) which remains a standard reference text for academics today, and a highly unconventional history of the church, *Descent of the Dove* (1939). Williams garnered a number of well-known admirers, including T. S. Eliot, W. H. Auden and C. S. Lewis. Towards the end of his life, he gave lectures at Oxford University on John Milton, and received an honorary MA degree. Williams died almost exactly at the close of World War II, aged 58.

[*From the Painting in the National Portrait Gallery*

THE EARL OF ROCHESTER
(Attributed to J. HUYSMANS)

Frontispiece]

CONTENTS

CHAP.		PAGE
I.	THE ROMANTIC FOREST	1
II.	THE EDUCATION OF A ROMANTIC	18
III.	THE ENGAGEMENT WITH DEATH	41
IV.	THE DUEL WITH MISS HOBART	56
V.	THE DUEL WITH LORD MULGRAVE	80
VI.	THE ACTOR AND THE THEATRE	115
VII.	INTERLUDES IN THE COUNTRY	154
VIII.	THE WAY OF SENSATION	170
IX.	THE WAY OF ARGUMENT	206
X.	THE WAY OF CONVERSION	242
XI.	THE WAY OF UNION	264
	INDEX	271

ACKNOWLEDGMENTS

THERE are three books on John Wilmot to which any student must be indebted—Mr. John Hayward's edition of the *Poems* (1926), Mr. Bonamy Dobree's *Rochester* (No. II. in the Second Series of Hogarth Essays, 1926), and the two volumes of researches by Herr Prinz (*John Wilmot* and *Rochesterians*). To these Professor V. de Sola Pinto has added a critical study in his recent book, *Rochester*; he has been good enough to discuss Rochester with me and to make of our separate tasks a pleasant companionship. Mr. Hayward has shown me many kindnesses; it is indeed a fortunate chance that has enlarged for me through this book the thing that Rochester and Burnet named as life's chief happiness—friendship. Mr. Francis Needham, by permission of the Duke of Portland, allowed me to see the manuscripts of poems by Rochester and Lady Rochester, which are shortly to be published.

CHAPTER I

THE ROMANTIC FOREST

IT was night when at last the Penderel brothers brought a ladder and the King of England came down from his tree. One of his few friends, a certain Colonel Careless, had been hidden with him all day in the branches; another, the Lord Wilmot, lay at a house some miles off. The remainder of the army, which three days before had been utterly defeated at Worcester, was either prisoner to Cromwell or fugitive through the countryside. Priests' holes were occupied in manor-houses; forgotten paths through the woods were retrodden. The Parliamentary horse searched roads and woods; about all the villages went rumours of the whereabouts of captain and colonel, and of the dark, tall, humorous creature of twenty-one, who stood now at the bottom of the ladder among his peasant saviours, the proclaimed public enemy, Charles Stuart.

The tree and the darkness, the descent and the subsequent flight, are the picturesque properties of a romantic tale. The scattered figures, escaping through the western counties, are the climax of defeat. They disappear along the roads, into London, into scattered manors, into small ships in remote harbours, and every way into obscurity. It is nine years before they, or their sons and inheritors, return. As again they approach, from foreign places, from statelier ships, from restored manors, a gaudier light abolishes the dim landscape of the forest of the flight. The palaces of Whitehall and St. James expand to receive them. Time and the world have changed.

The wood in which, on the evening of that Saturday, September 1651, Charles II. stood, was symbolical of another forest—a thing of the spirit. The King's was not the only English tree which had contained at times a mortal inhabitant. Four years before Worcester, in another part of the country, another young man of twenty-one, named George Fox, also took refuge in woods. He wrote of his own flight: " My troubles continued. . . . I fasted much and walked abroad in solitary places many days, and often took my Bible, and went and sate in hollow trees and lonesome places till night came on ; and frequently, in the night, walked mournfully about by myself : For I was a man of sorrows in the times of the first workings of the Lord in me."

He also was pursued ; unlike the King, he did not escape his pursuer. A spirit captured his spirit ; for him also the world changed. " Now was I come up in spirit, through the flaming sword, into the paradise of God. All things were new, and all the creation gave another smell unto me than before, beyond what words could utter."

The King escaped from his wood to temporal poverty, first in France, and afterwards in Whitehall ; George Fox to spiritual richness in the paradise of God. The one emerged into a state of dubious and difficult royalty, within as without ; the other, without as within, found a state of being of utter significance, of wholly desirable passion, and what he called " the hidden unity." The two exits were at opposite ends of that dark spiritual forest, in the maze of which were other wanderers, three of whom should be named.

One is of interest only as an historical coincidence. George Fox, interpreting his paradise into terms of mortal action, came to Derby, and there interrupted with vigorous theological protests a religious address by one of the military leaders of the Army of the Parliament. He was brought before the magistrates ; there was high controversy. The magistrates, Fox thought, were still roaming in the old entanglements of human language, opinion, and desire. They asked him if he were "sanctified." "I answered: 'Sanctified! yes,' for I was in the paradise of God. Then they asked me if I had no sin. I answered, 'Sin! Christ, my Saviour, has taken away my sin, and in Him there is no sin.' They asked how we knew that Christ did abide in us. I said, 'By His Spirit, that He has given us.' They temptingly asked if any of us were Christ. I answered, 'Nay, we are nothing, Christ is all.'" After which "for the avowed uttering and broaching of divers blasphemous opinions contrary to a late Act of Parliament," he was committed to prison, where he remained for a year.

In 1651 there came to Derby, marching on the way to Worcester, other regiments of the army; with them a certain soldier from Nottingham, by name Rice Jones. By accident he came into propinquity, and into argument, with the imprisoned Fox. It grieved Fox to discover that Rice Jones was a Gnostic; he altogether denied the objectivity of Christ's sufferings—there were never any such things happened; the history of the Passion was a mystical tale, to be understood mystically. Fox called these interpretations "imaginations and whimsies." The unmoved

Rice Jones marched on to Worcester with his company; it is pleasant to think that he, intensely concerned with his subjective transmutation, was one of those who rode under the tree where Charles Stuart, intensely aware of his own objective inconvenience, hid.

Rice Jones belonged to one of the wilder and more ancient tribes of the romantic spiritual forest. A fortnight after he had fought in the battle of Worcester, on Thursday, 18th September, while the King was resting in comparative comfort under the roof of a friend, a small boy, the son of an Edinburgh lawyer, kept his eighth birthday. His name was Gilbert Burnet; under the care of his father, a grave and slightly harsh practitioner of religion, he was already well advanced in the Latin tongue and the knowledge of classical authors. As he grew older, he read law and studied divinity. His divine studies led him, not to the obscure copses of Rice Jones's thought, or to the clear fields, beyond the forest, of Fox, or to the cleared spaces, on the hither side, of the scepticism of the King, but to one of the two great roads that then ran through the forest, the road of Anglican doctrine and the road of Roman doctrine. He became orthodox; he even became a bishop. More astonishingly, and less excusably, he came to believe that Christianity was rational. He had gone into the wilder retreats of the mystics, but had returned.

"The Misticks," he wrote, after reading St. Teresa and other such explorers, "being writ by recluse, melancholy people, . . . are full of rank enthusiasm."

He was a little surprised to find that his own close study of the Scriptures and religious discipline of life did not lead him with them into "all the extravagancies of Enthusiasme." He attributed his salvation from this danger to his having nothing of the spleen of melancholy in his constitution and to his philosophical studies. Philosophy taught him a certain disdain; it taught him to distinguish (he said) "between a heat in the animal spirits which was mechanicall, and that which lay in the superior powers of the soul."

In allusion to St. Teresa and George Fox, such a distinction is irrelevant enough. There are, however, less efficient travellers in the mystical depths than those two, and at least one of them was tamed by Gilbert Burnet's orthodox intelligence. Lady Henrietta Lindsay, daughter of the Countess of Balcarres, at the age of eighteen, fell into "histericall fits," in which she seemed to converse with God and the angels, and spoke, while the fit lasted, without interruption. It has been remarked that wiser visionaries allow God and the angels a greater share in the conversation than did the Lady Henrietta. One fit lasted ten hours; to the angels time is not so noticeable as to us. Burnet was called in; he advised her mother to send for a physician, and the fits ceased.

Yet Burnet was not without a longing for that stranger way. He practised asceticism; at one time he undervalued those who did not. He thought of abandoning the world, and of going unknown into a remote place to live and die, there to teach the poor. He desired mightily an " internal apprehension of extraordinary impulses," but he never found it. He had, in fact, a great number of romantic emotions, but philosophy and time subdued them. There remained in him only that enthusiasm which is the inevitable accompaniment of Christianity, the irrational creed warring with the scepticism which is at bottom all that philosophy can offer. At that time Descartes was writing in France, *cogito, ergo sum*, and begging the question with every word.

Another than Descartes had, in that same year 1651—the year of the King's escape, of Fox's release, of Gilbert Burnet's eighth birthday—in one great sentence, set an axe to the trunk of every tree in the wide romantic forest and, as it were, at the same time barred the high roads that ran through it. The young King, when he had been Prince of Wales, had had a mathematical tutor, by name Thomas Hobbes. In 1651 Thomas Hobbes published *Leviathan*. On the fifth page of that lucid work was the sentence which helped, both for good and evil, to set an age free from romantic vision and romantic entanglement. The sentence was : " Imagination is nothing but decaying sense." A little pallidly perhaps, and not with the full perfection of George Fox's day, its clarity breaks through the dark night of the soul. It freed those who walked in its light from much trouble ; it even justified them in not taking trouble. Hobbes removed vision and the intellect of vision, and for it he substituted the senses and the intelligence of the senses ; it is why he can never be neglected. It was he who, if he did not prepare the place, at least lit the candles in the palace of the consciousness of Whitehall. In that philosophical air he justified sensation to minds already eager for sensation. There were (he said) no motions in the soul. It is an historical and symbolical fact that Charles Stuart escaped from

England, driven by the military ardour and spiritual motions of Rice Jones and his comrades, to the city of Paris, where *Leviathan* had that year been published.

Among the peers and gentlemen who had followed the King to Worcester was Henry, Lord Wilmot. This lord was of a West Country family, of no very great standing; a man of gusto, enjoying his loyalty as he enjoyed his wine, and as apt to quarrel with his companions over the one as over the other. There is nothing to show that he ever cared much about the kind of tree to which George Fox retreated, but he was a gay and gallant companion of the lesser romanticism. He had accompanied Charles from the field, and after the main body of the King's companions had ridden off in other directions, he rode with him to Whiteladies, where the Penderels were. In their house, while the hasty discussions concerning disguise, flight, and safety went on, Henry Wilmot did his romantic best to assist them by setting to work to cut the King's long hair. It was significant devotion; it seems to have been no less significant that he did it badly, so that one of the woodcutters (perhaps more experienced—professional hairdressers were not in every hamlet) had to be called to finish it. On the Saturday which the

King spent in his tree, Wilmot lay in concealment in another house some miles away. On the Monday, the King set out to join him. When, again in the dim evening, they met the loyalist master of the house at the great door, Wilmot proclaimed to him the coming of the King in a fine phrase of rhetoric: "This is your master, my master, the master of us all."

The King, through the weeks that followed, went in disguise. Henry Wilmot, except for a hawk on his wrist, refused disguise. Certainly it was more necessary for Charles, who had the more noticeable figure—"almost two yards high," the Parliamentary proclamations called him. It is romantic that the King should have been disguised, and just as romantic that the Lord Wilmot should not. Sometimes together, sometimes separate, they rode on through those dangerous weeks towards the coast; and after them, in one form or another, rode the spiritual mystic, more deeply romantic than either—Serjeant Obadiah Bind-their-kings-in-chains-and-their-nobles-with-links-of-iron. The future, however—the intellectual future—was to be neither to the noble nor the Serjeant. Wilmot had left behind him, at his estate of Ditchley, in Oxfordshire, his wife and a young son, then four years old, John. When that child grew to manhood he was to find, for most of his life, his nearest kinship in the inverted romanticism of the King. But both Fox and Hobbes were to have their part in John Wilmot ; their great names describe different and contending states of his being. It was in the contention between those two states, and in the comment upon them of the third state, which can more properly be attributed to Charles Stuart, that the significance of John Wilmot's life was to lie.

When at last the little ship from Brighthelmstone containing Charles Stuart drew in to Normandy, the Lord Wilmot continued to be romantic in exile, though with little active success. He had, like Burnet, a mighty desire, but his gusto was for more possible things. The enthusiasms of the beggarly Court were for promises and titles. They asked of the King " very improper reversions because he could not grant the possession, and were solicitous for honours, which he had power to grant, because he had no fortunes which he could give to them." Henry Wilmot was solicitous to be an earl. The King, in those midnight wanderings and rests, had committed himself to warm gratitude to his companion. His companion desired the face value of those words to be justified. It is the disadvantage of kings and lovers that they are so held to their phrases. At first Wilmot asked no more than a general promise of an earldom some day—when it was convenient to the King. The King, grateful for the moderation, promised. Time betrayed him; presently, in the vagrant diplomacy of that vagrant Court, it seemed desirable to send an ambassador privately to the Diet of the Empire at Ratisbon. It was thought that the German princes might be willing to restore, to support, or at least to shelter, the King, since his more immediate brothers of France and Spain were by now rivals for the favour of the Lord Protector Cromwell. But there was no money to send an ambassador in formal state. Wilmot, seizing the opportunity, proposed that he should be made an earl and go privately. An English earl would be equal to any princes of the Empire, and he promised great results—reputation, money, men. The romantic desire of a title galloped level with the romantic dream of a Restoration; the Lord Wilmot indulged both emotions and found them satisfying. Charles had fewer hopes, but he yielded. The French Government, hoping to get Charles out of the country, supplied the money. Charles supplied the dignity and commission. Wilmot became Earl of Rochester, and the eight-year-old boy at Ditchley, in the custom of the English nobility, became in turn Lord Wilmot.

Wilmot was not the only messenger. Some years earlier the dramatist and (future) theatre manager, Sir Thomas Killigrew, had gone to Venice on something the same purpose. He had done his best; he had even published a full account of a great Royalist victory. Rather unfortunately, as things turned out, he put the scene of triumph at Worcester; months afterwards came the news of the actual battle, and ensured the underhand dismissal of the ambassador, in spite of the horrid reports of the Puritans which Killigrew had spread. He announced that St. Paul's Cathedral, "comparable with St. Peter's at Rome, remains desolate, and is said to have been sold to the Jews for a synagogue." He spoke of the publication of the Koran, "translated from the Turkish so that people may be imbued with Turkish manners, which have much in common with the actions of the rebels." It is true, no doubt, that Mahommedans, Jews, and Puritans all disliked images, but it seems unlikely that the Puritans fell back on the Koran as an incitement against idolatry. "Casting out Beelzebub by Beelzebub" could have no better example.

At Ratisbon the Earl of Rochester secured something like ten thousand pounds from some of the lesser princes. He spent a good deal on the negotiations; he made arrangements with old German officers; he plunged directly into the business of getting an army. It was, however, one thing to get an army; another, to pay it; a third, to use it. Edward Hyde, afterwards the Chancellor Clarendon, who disliked Rochester, commented gloomily: " So blind men are whose passions are so strong, and their judgments so weak that they can look but upon one thing at once." The Earl looked at least on two, as even Clarendon admitted. Having become Earl and been Ambassador, he looked to being Commander-in-Chief. In 1655 news reached the Court of all kinds of possibilities in England—risings in Kent, in the West, in the North. Rochester, signed commissions in his pocket, crossed to London. He was arrested on the way, and released; again arrested, and released; at last he was there. He sat among his friends, good fellows all, and anyone who was bold for the King and gallant with Henry Wilmot heard details of the risings. He sent off his companions, one to the West, one to the North. He wrote the most cheerful letters to the King, who allowed himself to become a little hopeful, and lay at Middleburgh ready to cross. Presently the Earl himself followed to the North. There, in Yorkshire, he became uneasy; preparations were not sufficiently advanced, prospects not sufficiently good. He and his allies " parted with little goodwill to each other," and the Earl set out on his return to London. " He departed very unwillingly from places where there was good eating and drinking "; he was nearly caught at Aylesbury. But the genius of his capacity for solitary romantic escapes stood by him and persuaded the innkeeper to assist him. He got away in time, lay for a while in London, and escaped at last back to Flanders and Cologne. It was his last adventure; in 1657 he died.

Charles Stuart, his romantic followers having failed him, found the realism of General Monk, of the Chancellor Hyde, and of the mass of the English, achieving at last the incalculable thing. The obscure forest of religious search, intellectual speculation, and romantic adventure receded. First London, then Whitehall, lay clear. Himself teased at once by a sceptical mind and an appetite for sensation, he was able to maintain a perilous superiority over the romantics and the antiromantics by whom he was, and was to be, surrounded. He was to walk sensitively on the borders of the forest of the spirit with a sardonic smile, not much different to that he gave to the suppers at which Lady Castlemaine soon provided him with the sensations of the flesh. Central to himself and determined not to yield that centre to the keeping of any romantic passion, he was content to allow romantic passion as much freedom as he conveniently could. Once at least in his life it got the better of him, when the evil of a romantic horror surged through London, and abandonment screamed round the gallows and shouted from the Bench in the iniquitous myth of the Popish Plot. Once, at the very end of his life, he submitted to a romantic glory, ordered and mediated through the classic instrument of the Roman Church. But both those moments were far off. Cosmopolitan and sceptical, he landed on the beach at Dover. With him, more by accident than design, and without any philosophical intensity, mediated through the desires of the Court, came the sensationalism of *Leviathan*. Its author had already composed his own sensations by making peace with Cromwell. The King was thirty. On the beach he embraced General Monk, and spoke to him beautifully as "Father." Before thousands of eyes the Mayor of Dover presented him with a copy of a volume full of the myths of the most extreme experiences of man, the Bible. The King looked at it and received it. " Mr. Mayor," says the King, emotionally handing it to one of the Court, " I love it above all things in the world."

CHAPTER II

The Education of a Romantic

JOHN WILMOT was born on 1st April 1647. Such a birthday has a kind of significance. It fits all of us, and John Wilmot especially, but only because he was fooled by Life rather more ostentatiously than most of us are. His genius assisted; his sensitive apprehensions summed up their thwarted desires in several of the most improper poems in the English language. The author of those poems on the failure of fruition, on "the imperfect enjoyment," on the indignant nymph and the impotent swain, was born in the same year in which George Fox seemed to himself to emerge from the entangled forest of the spirit into the paradise of "the hidden unity" which he found on the farther side.

Henry Wilmot had had no temptations to take refuge in a hollow tree from the celestial pursuit, nor had he ever been concerned with Hobbes's philosophical denial that the soul had motions in herself. He had been concerned with a world of more flagrant emotion. His wife, innocently, was related to the more fashionable world of sensation under the restored Monarchy. She was kindred to Barbara Villiers, afterwards Lady Castlemaine, the lurid and termagant mistress of Charles II.; "the most profane, imperious, and shameless of harlots," Macaulay called her, in a prose as shameless as his subject. Anne Wilmot was very different. She, like her husband Henry, came from the West Country; she, like him also, had been married before—to Sir Henry Lee, of Ditchley, in Oxfordshire. John was thus the son of second marriages on both sides. While Henry Wilmot went off to fight for and ride with his King and that King's heir, his own heir lived quietly at home. While Henry diplomatized in fairy-tales for Charles II., Anne devoted herself to the preservation of the estate and the protection of her son. She nourished them both excellently. She was a lady of a firm mind and not very wide sympathies; allusions in the later letters of her son to his wife suggest difficulties between Lady Wilmot and her daughter-in-law. She was a Puritan and the friend of Puritans, but the word covers a good deal; there is no reason to suppose she was harsh or austere. Her friend and co-guardian of the child, Sir Ralph Verney, was also Puritan by inclination, but he had fought on the King's side. In 1647 the lines of division between parties were changing every day, and the most intense desire of most of England was for a quiet life—with the King in possession, if possible; without, if there were no help for it. Lady Wilmot sat still, kept her soul, guarded her son, and hoarded her revenues.

John's horoscope was cast, and remains to us. " The sun governed the horoscope, and the moon ruled the birth hour." Lady of illusions, she did! " The conjunction of Venus and Mercury in M. coeli, in Sextile of Luna, aptly denotes his inclination to poetry." Perhaps, but in relation to the moon, mythical mistress of deceits, the conjunction of love and speed suggests, even more aptly, other characteristics. Venus indeed, most suitably " visible in full daylight," had adorned the day of Charles's birth; she and Mercury conjoined their effectiveness over many ladies and gentlemen of his court. They were the chief planets to rule over the ways that led from the dark forest of wandering minds to the palace of sensual delights. " The great reception of Sol with Mars and Jupiter posited so near the latter bestowed a large stock of generous and active spirits, which constantly attended on this excellent native's mind, so that no subject came amiss to him." Mars was to draw his active spirits to war with the Navy;

EDUCATION OF A ROMANTIC 21

Jupiter may have moved them to set up as a quack in Tower Street; it must have been the pride of Sol that so enraged his generous spirits as to allow them ungenerously to know of footmen with cudgels set in ambush for John Dryden.

In the education of her son Anne Wilmot had the assistance of Sir Ralph Verney, and of the Reverend Francis Giffard, her chaplain. Since, after the Revolution, Giffard was one of those who refused to take the oaths of allegiance to William and Mary, it is to be supposed that he too was a Royalist of strong principles. After his retirement he lived at Oxford, and there vented his reminiscences on the antiquary Thomas Hearne; it was then 1711, sixty years after he had educated John. He recounted, a little mysteriously, how he used "to lie with him in the family to prevent any ill accidents." The boy was then under twelve, for at twelve he left home for Oxford. Presumably Mr. Giffard succeeded, for he remembered his sometime charge as "very hopeful," "very virtuous and good-natur'd," "ready to follow good advice," "well-inclined to laudable undertakings." Hearne had heard different reports of John's later manhood. By 1711 John Wilmot had been dead for more than thirty years, but his reputation still burned. He was spoken of as "mad Rochester" and "the mad Earl." But the accounts of his childhood are all alike benign. He went from Mr. Giffard's teaching to the Grammar School at Burford. They found him extremely docile and extremely industrious. In Latin especially he was noted as being of extraordinary proficiency. It was a period when attention was paid to the distinguished young, and part of the attention was to see that they repaid the rest of it with all the diligence they could.

There is, however, no reason to doubt that the young John was both docile and industrious, an exemplary student. He was always apt to learn; the Court later found him as exemplary as had Mr. Giffard. He outwent his teachers and his examples—the Court, Cowley, Gilbert Burnet—all except the King. In such promise he went up, 15th January 1660, to Oxford, a fellow-commoner at Wadham.

It had originally been intended that Mr. Giffard should accompany him—so Mr. Giffard said—" and to have been his governor, but was supplanted." Mr. Giffard reluctantly abandoned Oxford and remained in the country, where the Countess of Rochester engaged earnestly in politics, being active to secure the return of her other son, Henry Lee, and Sir Ralph Verney to the Convention Parliament of 1660. At

Wadham the young Earl, under the care of the University authorities, pursued his studies. In May 1660 the first cloud of distraction appeared. Under the Protector's rule, the English weather had not been usually propitious to such clouds ; an overpowering sun of godliness threw a drought upon the land. With the return of Charles Stuart a thirsty people rejoiced. The King was up ; Puritanism was down. Loyalty and liberty came back, and riot ran to meet them. The King might love the Bible, as he told the Mayor of Dover, beyond all things in the world, but the English in general were very ready to love a number of other things almost as much. They had, for some years, been compelled to be monogamous to the Bible. Even at Oxford a little sensational polygamy was felt to be desirable. There were revels and riots. There were almost, in comparison with the past, orgies ; there were certainly delights, and they attracted John Wilmot. " He began to love these disorders too much." Till then he had had no disorders to love. The first chance, and still more the first sense, of outbreak, of a kind of communal outbreak, ran across his quick and vivid mind. He was just thirteen. He had docilely explored Latin and the great classics. At the moment when his own sense of liberty and power was growing in him it was met by a sudden enthusiasm of liberty and power from without. The King's return meant all this, and accidentally it meant something more. John Wilmot was now, by his father's death, Earl of Rochester; he was the son of the King's friend. It meant a good deal more now than it could have done before. He had been taught loyalty, but now he was in possession of lordship. His family and his University had exalted the person of the King; all the nation rejoiced in the person of the King. He was—and at thirteen in the seventeenth century he must have known it—one of those who had access, in the due future, to the Court and the person of the King. Many were looking forward to place and title, but he had a title already, and could have a place.

He produced a poem, or so it was said. It was also said later that one of his tutors, Dr. Whitehall (prophetic name!), a physician, of Merton, had actually produced it, and affixed his pupil's name to it. It seems almost certain that Dr. Whitehall had a hand in it, so advanced is it for thirteen years, even the thirteen years of the seventeenth century. The opening quatrain has in it something of the last mad metaphors of the metaphysical poets. It may be hoped, and perhaps believed, that the future "mad Earl" wrote a good deal of it. His wildness was always akin to theirs, and he admired Cowley, we know. Cowley might have written :

> Vertue's triumphant Shrine! who dost engage
> At once three Kingdoms in a Pilgrimage ;
> Which in ecstatick Duty strive to come
> Out of themselves, as well as from their home.

So the Earl, or his tutor, addressed Charles. Dryden, on the same occasion, was plunging as wildly into a similar religious metaphor. He assured the King

> It is no longer Motion cheats your view,
> As you meet it, the Land approacheth you.
> The Land returns, and in the white it wears
> The marks of Penitence and Sorrow bears.

So useful to poets are the white cliffs of Dover. But the comparison of Charles to a triumphal shrine of virtue had even less exactitude of detail to recommend it. If Rochester wrote it, it was his first poem to the King, and the last in that particular style. His later addresses were quite different. The conclusion of his poem differed from Dryden's. The greater John had written an earlier poem upon the death of the Lord Protector, to which he did not now refer. He contented himself with saying that the world would now have a monarch, " and that Monarch *You.*" (The italics are Dryden's.) But Rochester was able to end by recalling, if not his own past, at least his father's; he alluded (great SIR) to Henry Wilmot's "daring loyalty." Perhaps at the moment Charles preferred Dryden's, if he saw either; there were too many recollections of daring loyalties appearing in hopeful joy about his path.

Dr. Whitehall seems to have been an actual example of the semi-fabulous, less reputable, Church of England clergyman of the time. He had been brought up at Westminster under the great Busby, and had thence become a student of Christ Church. In 1648, at a parliamentary visitation, he was asked whether he would submit to their authority, and answered:

> My name's Whitehall, God bless the poet,
> If I submit the King shall know it.

Provoked by the royalism and unplacated by the rhyme, the visitors turned him out. In 1650, however, he came back, this time to Merton, as a Fellow. It was commonly reported that he had gained this favour by subservience to the Ingoldsby family, who were his neighbours in the country, and especially to Richard Ingoldsby, the regicide, "before whom he often acted the part of a mimic and buffoon on purpose to make him merry." The riotous heart of Whitehall proceeded to occupy itself with physic and poetry. He remained in favour with the Government, being made a Doctor of Physic in 1657 at the letters of Richard Cromwell, then chancellor of Oxford. He produced a number of Latin poems in honour of Oliver Cromwell, Richard Cromwell, King Charles II., and Lord Clarendon ; and certain English poems of quite another type.[1] He produced one poem to his pupil Rochester, sent with a portrait of himself, from which we gather that he had, in a practical way, assisted his pupil's levity as well as his learning :

> Tis not in vest, but in that gowne
> Your Lordship daggled through this towne
> To keep up discipline, and tell us
> Next morning where you found good-fellows.

It ends with a jest, more dexterous than decent, and was sent to the Earl five years later, on New Year's Day 1666/7.

Under such instruction, therefore, Rochester resumed his studies, with docility if not with

[1] He was concerned in an exchange of verse with one Edmund Gayton, " superior beadle of arts and physic," who was likewise turned out by the visitors, but (less fortunate than Whitehall) did not get back until after the Restoration and had to live by his wits in London. It was after the death of Mr. Gayton in 1666 that the great Dr. Fell, at a convocation held to elect his successor in the beadleship, " exhorted the masters in a set speech to have a care whom they should choose, and desired them by all means that they would not elect a poet, or any that do *libellos scribere.*"

enthusiasm, and with sufficient industry to allow him in the autumn of 1661 to take his M.A. The ceremony of bestowal of degrees was that year presided over by a great personage—the Chancellor of the University who was also Chancellor of England, the Lord Edward Hyde, Earl of Clarendon. He was something even more than this, though dangerously and against his will, for his daughter Anne had but lately married the heir-presumptive to the Throne, James, Duke of York. This figure of ancient loyalty, which was now by that marriage almost a figure of semi-royalty, and yet was already beginning to appear to the younger courtiers in London a mere figure of fun, sat in the high seat and ceremonially shook hands with the young Masters, among whom was his own third son Edward, then about seventeen. As the slender figure of the fourteen-year-old Earl, *Dominus Rochester*, appeared before him, some sudden tenderness moved the old man: a recollection of days of exile when Henry Wilmot and he, antipathetic though they may have been, shared a common poverty in Paris, or an apprehension of the restored world into which the young heir of Wilmot was advancing. He distinguished the boy, it was remarked, by a special grace; he held his hand, drew him near, kissed his left cheek, and dismissed him with special benignity. With the presentation, in the next year, of four silver pint-pots to Wadham, my lord's connexion with the University closed.

In 1662 or thereabouts my lord went abroad. His governor was a certain Dr. Balfour—also, like Dr. Whitehall, a physician. They passed through Paris, France, Italy. He was at Padua during October 1664. Europe was everywhere turning from the darkness of the Wars of Religion to the cooler and clearer age of Louis XIV., the boy who was on the point of assuming the government of France into his own hands. The form of Louis stands at the entrance to one of the highroads through that aged forest of men's imaginations, the high road of the Roman clarity of dogma upon which so much of the culture of Europe walked—a road barred in England to all but a minority of obstinate devoted souls, and regarded by others, equally devoted, such as John Bunyan in his prison at Bedford, as not much unlike a direct pathway to hell. With such things John Wilmot was not concerned. He gathered up his experiences, his adolescence took on the bright colour of courtliness and the gentle hardihood of Courts; and—more interestingly—he returned, in that courtly grace, to his first love. Compulsion had neighboured his boyhood with learning; he began now to woo her of his own will.

It seems to have been Dr. Balfour's work. When the two started, Rochester had not quite recovered from his too much love of those Restoration disorders. He was an official Master of Arts, and that was all. Dr. Balfour set himself to invigorate that mastery, and, on Rochester's own showing, succeeded. In the midst of the polite world of Europe, study came again to her own. Certainly that world encouraged it; letters were still a habit of thought in the high ranks of society. Even so, the world was full of a number of things. Balfour quickened Wilmot's knowledge of one group. My lord's mind, naturally vivid, became more eager. He was disposed to a habit of intelligence and even of philosophy. He was prepared to come to conclusions.

So acquainted with the world of men—men in their books and men in their behaviour; so prepared for whatever his own English world, at its shining centre, had to offer him of loyalty, of learning, of poetry, of love; delicately metaphysical, sensitively expectant, he returned. There was in him, as in Gilbert Burnet away in Scotland, a formative desire for " an intimate apprehension of extraordinary impulses," natural to youth, but especially strong in this youth.

EDUCATION OF A ROMANTIC 31

He had (they say) at this time a rare and striking modesty; he was docile to the impulses of the world. So prepared, at seventeen years old, tall and slender, well-bred, capacious of experience, he returned. In the year 1665 he made his first appearance in the galleries of Whitehall.

From that day my lord's life is shown us by a series of momentary flashes rather than in continuous sequence. It is even impossible to be certain of the proper order of all the flashes. Some are dated, some are approximately dated, some are not dated at all. Most of his letters are undated. Nevertheless, the dates we have suggest the possibility of a pattern; even though the pattern must be less justified than in most biographies, it may be as just as most. Picture after picture is flung swiftly before us, until we reach the last more detailed picture of his death. In all there is an energy, an energy which seems to have become almost terrible to the Court in which he moved, an energy of search for something he could not find, an energy of anger and contempt for what, in himself as in others, he did find. He desired significant emotion; they offered him insignificant sensation. He loved it, but felt himself thwarted by it, and they grew afraid of him. Like George Fox among the preachers, like the Fifth Monarchy men in the City, Lord Rochester ravaged his unmeaning contemporaries in a search for meaning. They called him "the mad Earl." His actions provoked the phrase, but his hunger provoked his actions. He desired, like all romantics, a justified passion. In the days of the King's father and grandfather, it would have been more easy to find. Those good, or evil, days were past. A schism was opening in the English imagination : on the one side Fox and Wesley, on the other Pepys and Walpole. The courtiers of heaven and the courtiers of Whitehall were becoming divided, not only in their conduct but in their idealism. The saint and the gentleman and their less intelligent disciples—fanatics and prigs, debauchees and good fellows—were beginning to be at odds. By a trick of Fate Lord Rochester ignorantly found himself on the wrong side. He belonged to the gentlemen, but he was a romantic, and they were not romantic. When romantics cannot find the world they desire, they yearn to create it. The Lord Rochester found, or created, his—on his death-bed.

The details of the Court in which he carried on his search may be postponed until his second arrival at it after two adventures of love and war. On his first appearance he was an immediate success. The King and Lady Castlemaine were gracious. The gentlemen were delightful; the ladies were kind. The Court was always willing to welcome handsome and entertaining postulants of its pleasures. At first John Wilmot was not remarkably different from most of the others, unless indeed it may be taken as a difference that an early and notorious exhibition of action was aimed at marriage rather than simple seduction. Since the lady was an heiress there were reasons for marriage, but there were perhaps others.

In 1665 he was eighteen; it was the year of the Plague, but in May this had hardly begun to appear. There was in London a young woman of good family and, as things went then, good income, Elizabeth Mallet. She was the daughter of John Mallet, a West Country gentleman, and granddaughter of a peer, Lord Hawley. She belonged, therefore, to the outer circle of the Families—those Families who were by now circumscribing the King and hampering the administration of the King's Government. There were a number of suitors. Elizabeth had promised not to marry without the consent of her people—her father, mother, and grandfather. She had, however, also declared that she would "choose for herselfe." The Lord John Butler, the Lord Desmond's son, the Lord Hinchingbrooke, were competing for her. The last was the son of the Earl of Sandwich, Pepys's superior, Admiral of the Narrow Seas, Lieutenant Admiral to the Duke of York, and Master of the Wardrobe. Sandwich pushed his son's suit; there was a kind of understanding. But a greater than Sandwich indicated his pleasure. The King recommended John Wilmot to the attention of Elizabeth.

He had been approached to this end by two personages who, themselves enemies, were united by the requests of the young courtier. Lord Clarendon and Lady Castlemaine had been approached. They both proposed the match to the King. It might have had political advantages. The Lord Rochester was young, he was not under the influence of a father, and there was in his house a tradition of devoted loyalty. Henry Wilmot might not have been much good as the King's servant, no more good than Clarendon had thought him. Sandwich, however, had been definitely Cromwell's man, and though all those unhappy old divisions had been healed, it cannot have seemed an unwise thing to Charles to attach Rochester to himself and a fortune to Rochester. The more strength of men and money the King could have for his privy servants the better. He needed all the counter-weight he could find to the enlarging power of the Families.

In December 1664, Sandwich, saying that he would not go against the King's pleasure, withdrew. But either Elizabeth herself or her guardians were still discontented with Lord Rochester. In view of all the events, it is most likely that it was the guardians. At the beginning of May, " my lord of Rochester is encouraged by the King to make his addresses to Mrs. Mallet." Since the lady was not averse, and since the King was certainly favourable, the young romantic determined to act. At the end of May the Plague had begun to appear, and the Dutch War was in progress. Sandwich was away at sea with the Fleet, commanding the Blue, under the Duke of York. On Friday, 24th May, Elizabeth Mallet came to supper at Whitehall with Frances Stewart, whom gossip asserted to be Lady Castlemaine's chief rival. Supper ended, the ladies parted. Elizabeth entered a coach, in the company and guard of her grandfather Lord Hawley, a man of fifty-seven. It rolled off towards Charing Cross. There, in the twilight, stood another coach, one with six horses. As they came level, sudden voices and noises broke out. The coach was stopped violently; the door was forcibly opened; Elizabeth was invited to descend. Despite Lord Hawley, she was compelled to obey; she was hurried over to the other coach. Two women received her. As soon as she had well entered, the vehicle began to move. She was swept off into the night. Lord Rochester himself, the abduction accomplished, took horse and rode gaily north.

Lord Hawley was more successful in speeding the pursuit than in preventing the seizure. It is to be supposed that he hurried back at once to the palace. Horsemen went out after Rochester, and caught him at Uxbridge. The lady was not so soon discoverable. On the Sunday, 26th May, the tale was about the town. Pepys took it to Lady Sandwich, the wife of his patron. He was able to assure her, to her pleasure, that the King was very angry, and was sending the Earl to the Tower. On the Monday, in fact, warrants flew out. It was the earliest opportunity; on Saturday the news had come too late. A warrant ordered Lord Rochester's conveyance to the Tower; another, his reception there; another, search after the armed men who assisted him, and aid from all men in the still unsuccessful search after Mistress Mallet. Somewhere—perhaps Rochester himself revealed the place; it was of no service to him to defy the King from his Tower prison—she was found and brought back.

Lord Rochester, all agreed, had made his throw and lost. "By consent of all," wrote Pepys, "my lord Hinchingbrooke stands fair, and is invited for her." Lady Sandwich, in considerable nervous excitement, remained in London, against her will. The sickness in the City was spreading, and she was afraid of it. Eleven days later, she was still there. By then news had reached her from sea that the fleets were engaged, and from town that doors were already closed and marked with the red cross of the Plague and the dreadful appeal, *Lord, have mercy upon us.* Alarmed for her husband and herself, she was compelled to tarry in hope for her son, "my lord Rochester [being] now declaredly out of hopes of Mrs. Mallet."

But within four days after his committal to the Tower, before the end of May, Lord Rochester was petitioning to be let out. He apologized; he implored. His offence, he said charmingly, was due to "inadvertence, ignorance of the law, and passion." He would rather have died ten thousand deaths than incurred His Majesty's displeasure. The King kept him prisoner for almost a fortnight. On 9th June he was released on condition that he surrendered himself to a Secretary of State on the first day of Michaelmas term. Before then he had not only regained but increased his favour. At first, however, he did not remain at Court.

The Duke of York returned with Lord Sandwich and the Fleet, victorious from the battle of Lowestoft; and when, late in July, this time under Sandwich's sole command, the Fleet stood out to sea again, Lord Rochester went with it. The Plague grew, and became sensational, and the great folk fled, and it abated, and they returned. Nell Gwynn appeared for the first time on the stage at Drury Lane in an insignificant part in John Dryden's *Indian Emperor,* premonitory of the insignificant sensations she was to cause in the King. The Fleet came back, and went out again. More than a year after her abduction, Elizabeth, still unmarried, was discussing her suitors. In February 1666 " a servant of hers " proposed to Sandwich something like an elopement : " to compass the thing without respect of friends, she herself having a respect to my Lord's family, but my Lord will not listen to it but in a way of honour." In August she had Hinchingbrooke in attendance on her at Tunbridge Wells, but they found each other less than agreeable, " she declaring her affections to be settled, and he not being fully pleased with the vanity and liberty of her carriage." By the end of November she was still discussing them. "My lord Herbert," she had said, "would have her; my lord Hinchingbrooke was indifferent to have her; my lord John Butler might not have her; my lord Rochester would have forced her; and Sir (Francis) Popham (who nevertheless is likely to have her) would do any thing to have her." Suddenly she yielded. At least my Lord Rochester had done something; she married him on 29th January 1666/7. A few days afterwards, both Frances Stewart and the Earl and Countess were at the play. The audience in the pit saw them and chattered: "It is a great act of charity, for he hath no estate."

The business of Miss Mallet's estate caused some difficulty. There were negotiations. In the country the Dowager Countess appealed again to Sir Ralph Verney, writing that "the King I thank god is very well satisfyed with it, & they had his consent when they did it—but now we are in some care how too get the estate, they are come too desire to parties with friends, but I want a knowing frind in business, such a won as Sr Raph Varney."

But the possible implication was false. If Elizabeth Mallet married at all for charity, it was for that pure goodwill which is so often felt in the first exchanges of romantic love. Years afterwards, her husband, writing to her, could say that her entire revenue " has hithertoo, and shall (as long as I can gett bread without it) bee wholly imploy'd to the use of yr self and those who depend on you; if I prove an ill Steward att least you never had a better, wch is some kind of satisfaction to Your humble Servant."

CHAPTER III

THE ENGAGEMENT WITH DEATH

BEFORE, however, the experience of marriage opened on Rochester, he had endured a definite defeat of the spirit. He had made, in the metaphysical fury of his adolescence, a demand on the universe which had been refused. Like the Court of King Charles, the court of heaven delayed my lord's imperious request, nor was he allowed to abduct his desire.

He had been in the Tower when the Duke of York brought back the Fleet from his and its victory over the Dutch at the battle of Lowestoft in June 1665. The possible complete destruction of the Dutch Fleet had been prevented by the deliberate lies of the Duke's gentleman-in-waiting, Mr. Brouncker. When, after the battle, the Duke—to whom, as Admiral-in-Chief, the credit was and is due—retired to get some rest, Brouncker went up to the captain of the flagship and told him the Admiral's commands were to shorten sail, and thus check the pursuit of the flying enemy. The captain answered that he had the Admiral's instructions to maintain the pursuit and dare not disobey except on equally explicit instructions from the same source. Brouncker went below, waited a few moments, and went up again with the definite statement that the Duke commanded the ship to shorten sail. It was false, but it was believed. The enemy got away. The Fleet returned to England to refit.

By the end of June it was ready for another expedition. This time it was to be aimed at the Dutch Admiral, De Ruyter, who was returning from the East Indies with treasure ships. But this time the High Admiral was denied the command, since it was thought undesirable that the life of the heir-presumptive should be continually risked in sea-fights. The Fleet was put into the charge of Sandwich, who had joined it on 1st July. The King was on the *Royal Charles* on that day; a final council was held. The King returned to London, and presently from London, among other charges and instructions, there arrived at the Fleet, as a gentleman volunteer, the Earl of Rochester, bearing a personal letter of recommendation from the King.

He wrote later to his mother: " It was not fitt for mee to see any occasion of service to the King without offering my self, so I desired and obtained leave of my Ld. Sandwich to goe with them." It must be admitted that he had not felt the same impulse of loyalty when the Fleet had originally sailed early in May. Elizabeth Mallet is certainly a reason; he had there an occasion of service to himself, and a romanticism of love instead of war. Elizabeth Mallet, for the time being, was out of reach; the King would not consent to show such extreme placability towards the fond lover as a continued countenancing of his suit would have meant. Neither, however, would Charles encourage Lord Hinchingbrooke. Lady Sandwich had been disappointed. She lay ill at Tonbridge, and the King commended one disappointed lover to the care of another disappointed lover's father. It seems likely that he derived an intellectual sensation of pleasure from the act.

Sandwich had just succeeded, through the good offices of Pepys, in arranging the marriage of his daughter Jemima to Philip Cartaret, son of Sir George Cartaret, Treasurer of the Navy, with unusually good financial results. He received his son's rival with courtesy. "In obedience to your Majesty's commands by my Lord Rochester, I have accommodated him the best I can, and shall serve him as best I can." The young man—he was now eighteen—was sent off to the *Royal Katherine*, and the Fleet set sail.

It was hoped, by the King, the Duke of

York, Sandwich, and a few others, that its business might be easier than seemed probable. Victories on the open sea against the Dutch Fleet were very well, but victories with a minimum risk were still better. Negotiations were in progress with the King of Denmark, who was also King of Norway. If De Ruyter took refuge in a Danish harbour, it was proposed that that King should permit an attack on them there; he was offered half the spoil as inducement, and sufficient secrecy to "cover it from the world." The King was supposed to have agreed. The English ambassador at Copenhagen reported that he "had ordered his Governor to shoot only powder"; presently he added that the Governor was not to shoot at all, only "to storm and seem to be highly offended." Cartaret understood even more, that the King of Denmark had promised "to doe great matters against that Nation." Letters went to Sandwich assuring him that, beyond protest, no action would be taken against the English ships if they attacked the Dutch in a Danish harbour.

By the end of July Sandwich heard that the treasure fleet was in the harbour of Bergen. He detached Sir Thomas Teddiman, with fourteen ships, to attack them. Rochester transferred to one of them, the *Revenge*, since the great *Royal*

THE ENGAGEMENT WITH DEATH 45

Katherine was not to go; it was supposed there would be no need to venture her. With him went Sandwich's son Sydney Montagu, his cousin Edward Montagu, John Windham, and other gentlemen volunteers—the last two had certainly also been on the *Revenge*. They, like the Kings of England and Denmark, parted the lion's skin, more gaily than the royal hunters. Three days afterwards, on 3rd August, the young poet wrote an account of the whole business to his mother, with a flourish, " from the coast of Norway, amongst the rocks, aboard the *Revenge*." There he spoke of the division. " Some for diamonds, some for spices others for rich silkes and I for shirts and gould wch I had most neede of, but reckoning without our Hoast wee were faine to reckon twice." The jest was literal. The Danish host did not prove as hospitable as had been expected. His churlishness ruined the calculations of the King, the hopes of the Admiral, and the more airy fantasies of the gentlemen volunteers.

The English Fleet reached Bergen on 1st August, and entered the harbour, through the narrow roadstead between the cliffs. The Dutch ships were lying, " incapable of execution." The English took up their position " close to the Dutch ships in the port and under the Castle."

Night fell. The three gentlemen on the *Revenge*—Edward Montagu, John Windham, and John Wilmot—talked together, and their talk was full of presentiments of death. Death certainly was near them. The city they had left but a few weeks before had been filling with it; the perils of the sea on which they sailed threatened it; the battle of the morrow promised it. A darker presentiment than such natural accidents possessed two of them. Edward Montagu said he was sure he should not return to England; he was quite certain he should not. Windham admitted he was half persuaded of a similar fate. Less certain than Montagu, he yet looked forward to death. Lord Rochester heard them; the romanticism of night and sea and battle was around him; and the agnosticism of the future. In a ceremony of solemn oaths he determined to bind death to his will. Montagu, more convinced than the others of his immediate end, would have no part in it; he separated his soul. But Rochester and Windham, under the high Danish castle, the guns yet silent, made an agreement between themselves that if indeed either died, and found himself in any future state, he should appear once more to his friend and declare the truth. Between sky and sea they made their covenant, and confirmed it with " ceremonies of religion "—vows and invocations of God. The dawn came nearer; they went to their duties. The bond of mutual apparition lay close to Rochester's heart.

Edward Montagu's last duty, before the battle began, was to pay a visit to the Danish Governor. All night messengers had been rowing forwards and backwards to the Castle. The Governor had protested against the entrance of so many ships. The English grew slowly convinced that this was not the mere noise with which they had been threatened. Action was being taken, not only on board the Dutch ships but in the Castle. Cannon, powder and shot, and Dutch sailors, were being got ashore and into position. The Dutch ships of the convoy were moved into better places; their broadsides trained on the invaders. The Castle fired a shot as a warning, which broke the leg of an English sailor. The Governor demanded time to communicate with Copenhagen. The English Admiral refused. He sent a last message by Montagu, offering (report said) the Garter. The Governor remained unpersuaded, and preparations for battle went swiftly on. Teddiman called his captains, held a last council, and then, giving them orders not to fire at the Castle, commanded the "fighting colours" to be broken, and let fly his broadside at the Dutch Fleet. The Castle immediately replied. The battle began at dawn ; after three hours, before it was yet full morning, the English were compelled to retire.

The smoke was blown by the wind over the English ships. During the struggle something over a hundred men were killed, six captains, and a few of the gentlemen-volunteers. Sidney Montagu, Sandwich's son, fell. On the *Revenge* the three gentlemen had taken their full part, exposed but unhurt. Towards the end of the battle, Windham, when they were all close together, was seized by a fit of giddiness. He reeled, he almost fell ; Montagu caught him. Rochester saw it. In the moment when the two so stood, a single doom was upon them. A Dutch ball struck them both, killing Windham outright and so terribly wounding Montagu that he died within the hour. Did the chance of things attend to men's minds, it might at least, for the mere sake of being exact to their presentiments, have ordered their deaths the opposite way.

In his next day's letter, from " among the rocks," Rochester told his mother of this ; of the covenant between spirits he said nothing. But he waited, he expected ; by an intolerant romanticism he demanded that death and supernature should accede to mortal bonds. He

THE ENGAGEMENT WITH DEATH 49

expected a vision. No vision came. The grave remained oblivious of his need. He had felt, in their talk, a kind of divination of spirit; "the soul had presages." He had seemed to find a greatness of significant emotion—emotion significant of death and life after death. Days went by; weeks. His emotion remained unjustified. For all the revelation that came, that hour of dark and thrilling engagement might as well not have been. At last he abandoned expectation; there was no hope here of justifying to himself his own capacity of passion. The death of Windham offered him no personal greatness of immediate experience.

Yet the sense of presage remained. Desiring to attach importance to his emotions, he overvalued them. Coincidence existed, but he desired palpable drama. He had a passion for drama, and he desired the unseen world to provide him with a theatre greater than that of the actual world, as that provided a finer than the King's Playhouse in Drury Lane. He was never a poseur, but he was always an actor. It was his misfortune that the Court of Charles Stuart offered him no adequate dramatic parts. He tried to create them even there; he ran from it to create them; anything that was offered him anywhere he was always ready to take. He waited always for his cue, ready to improvise, capable of any gallant and romantic improvisation. The universe neglected his cue. Panting and willing, he waited in the wings, and the right recognizable words never came. Yet he felt them through his wild heart, felt them being spoken, and could not guess where.

At some later date his ardour for supernatural confirmation, for a suitable dramatic resolution of a dramatic crisis, was again excited. It was in the house of his wife's people, the Mallets of Shropshire. The chaplain of the family had a dream that on a certain day he would die. He recounted it to the household, by whom, naturally, he was rallied on his superstition. Their mockery or his own piety rebuked him; half-ashamed, he put it from his mind, and the day approached without his remarking it. On the eve he came into supper. A party of twelve were already gathered; he entered and took his place, the fatal thirteenth. One of the young ladies present noticed the number. She stretched out her arm, pointing at the chaplain, crying out that it was he who would die. He recollected his dream ;. the accident seemed to confirm it; he sat "in some disorder." A gleam of the supernatural from George Fox's world of portents and miracles flashed across the rational dining-room of John Mallet. The Earl [1] looked at the distracted chaplain; certainly the soul had presages. Mrs. Mallet rebuked her spiritual director, but the thing had too much hold for him to fear his patroness's disdain. He answered that he was sure he should die before morning. They all looked at him, sitting there in perfect health, and tossed the moment's joke aside. "It was not much minded," Rochester said; perhaps none but he and the victim cared. It was Saturday night. On the next day the chaplain was to preach. Presently he withdrew, to work at his sermon in his own room by candle-light. There on the Sunday morning they found him, his candle burnt down, his manuscript spread before him, inexplicably dead.

"These things," my lord said afterwards, "made me inclined to believe the soul was a substance distinct from matter." It was the adequate inclination of his mind; his heart laboured with a riddling desire. "Le cœur," Pascal was writing in France, "a ses raisons que la raison ne connait point." But with the logic of the intellectual heart Rochester was not well acquainted. That needs the imagination which is the companion of spiritual love, as

[1] It is not certain he was there. But he told the story as if he had been.

Wordsworth, a poet who was something more than a romantic, has taught us. Behind and before Rochester went the masters of those terrifying syllogisms, the syllogisms which are as much of the blood as of the brain. But another master intervened ; " imagination was nothing else but the decay of sense." And Fox, who might have been an interpreter, provincial as he was, was distant, in space and social degree, from my lord. John Wilmot's heart throbbed ; " presagefully it beat ; presagefully." He could not follow the presages. Something seemed to have been spoken, but not to him.

The visit to the Mallets is undated ; it seems probable that it took place after his marriage in 1667. Meanwhile his temporal affairs prospered better than his spiritual. He had returned to the King from his first experience of a double defeat—by the Danes and by the Deity—in September 1665. Lord Sandwich, writing dispatches, referred Charles for particulars to Lord Rochester, " who was present, and showed himself brave, industrious, and of useful parts." At the end of October, Charles bestowed £750 on Lord Rochester, " without account, as the King's free gift." By the next March he was sworn Gentleman of the Bedchamber.

In July he was at sea again, and involved in

THE ENGAGEMENT WITH DEATH 53

the battle of 25th July—St. James's Fight, off the mouth of the Thames. The fighting was fiercer than at Bergen. The gentlemen-volunteers lost heavily; one died in Rochester's arms. He had achieved a reputation for courage and a cool head in the Bergen battle. One of the volunteers, Sir Thomas, afterwards Lord Clifford, had spoken highly of his behaviour. He renewed it in his second affair. His immediate commander, Sir Edward Spragge, desired to send a special message to one of the captains with whose action he was dissatisfied. Smoke veiled the signals. It became necessary to lower a boat. Spragge asked for a volunteer; there was a momentary hesitation, in which the Earl offered himself. His offer was accepted. He passed safely through the shot, delivered his message, and safely returned. The action was "much commended by all who saw it."

With that, suddenly, his naval activities ceased. He came back to the Court, being now nineteen, and, so restored to the royal favour, resumed, more discreetly, his pursuit of Miss Mallet. In January 1667 he married her. In March he took up his duties as a Gentleman of the Bedchamber, taking the place of the Duke of Buckingham. He was given, at any rate officially, a troop of horse, and there is some slight reason to think he may have been on duty in June when the Dutch ships were proceeding to the Medway.¹ The warrant for his captaincy in Prince Rupert's Horse is dated 13th June 1667, the day on which the fireships were already in Chatham harbour, and the Duke of Albemarle (formerly General Monk) was hastily organizing the defence. On the previous day the Dutch had entered the river. It is permissible to speculate on a hasty volunteering and at least some hasty willingness to fight. But in general he did no more. He was married; he was in favour; he had tasted the sensations of battle, and now the sensations of the Court were more attractive. Romantic emotions of death had remained unjustified; a realistic sensationalism was a more immediately pleasing thing. There is little to show that he regarded patriotism or the service of the State as a possibly significant

¹ In 1681, during the King's vengeance on the perpetrators of the Popish Plot, a certain Stephen College was put on trial for high treason. During the trial the following dialogue took place. A witness from Watford, College's birthplace, called to testify to his character, said: "I knew him a soldier for his majesty, in which service he got a fit of sickness which had like to have cost him his life; he lay many months ill, to his great charge." Serjeant (afterwards Judge) Jeffries asked: "Where was it he was in his majesty's service?" and the witness answered: "At Chatham business." The prisoner added: "It was under my lord Rochester." But in 1681 there was another Rochester, Laurence Hyde; it may have been he that was meant.

emotion. What he wanted, so far as he could, he always took, and he was at liberty to take it now. At least he had shown his courage; it has some bearing on later incidents in his life.

On 21st July 1667 peace was signed at Breda. The King, the Court, and the Earl were free to devote themselves more assiduously to politics, poetry, philosophy, wine, riot, and love.

CHAPTER IV

THE DUEL WITH MISS HOBART

AT some time in those early months at Court, the first social comedy in which Lord Rochester is recorded to have played a part took place. Its exact date is uncertain; it must have been before the end of 1666, when one of the other characters was married and went down to a sedate wedded life in the country. A possible and convenient date would be the early part of 1666, when the Earl was at Court between his two sea-battles, and when he was, for the time being, still out of the royal favour for the favours of Elizabeth Mallet, or the lady had not been persuaded to bestow her own. This comedy then took place between the melodramas of death. It is true that we owe our account of it entirely to Anthony Hamilton, who, when he wrote the *Memoirs of the Count de Grammont*, regarded himself as an artist rather than as a scholar, and made of facts whatever his taste chose. If we can at all believe it, we must observe Rochester as already—at nineteen—a person of importance, a delight and a terror. He had always an interest in the theatre, and his best part was always himself. It is likely, however, that Hamilton exaggerated—perhaps even invented. But, unless and until we know more, the story cannot be omitted.

The other chief personage in the comedy is a Miss Hobart. Miss Hobart had been one of the Maids of Honour of the Duchess of York, Anne Hyde, daughter of the old Earl of Clarendon. Miss Hobart's shape was good, her wit sufficient, and she had " rather a bold air." More unusually, in that Court, she had a passion for the company of ladies. There had been an intense friendship, and afterwards a coolness, between her and another Maid of Honour, a Miss Bagot. Miss Bagot was the first to withdraw; she let it be understood that she was unable satisfactorily to encounter the warmth of Miss Hobart's affections. Miss Hobart was observed to be solacing herself with the company of a young girl, the niece of the Mother of the Maids of Honour. The Court engaged in agreeable speculation upon Miss Hobart's loves and capacities, and composed verses upon her; the Maids, innocently or scandalously, exhibited reluctance to be intimate with her. Tales came to the ears of the Duchess, who was incredulous, indignant, and embarrassed.

The Mother of the Maids, who had at first

been delighted that Miss Hobart should take notice of her niece, became agitated, and consulted the feline grace of Lord Rochester concerning the danger run by the poor girl among Miss Hobart's cushions. Lord Rochester sympathized, and offered his services. Presently the niece, whose name is given as Sarah Cooke, felt the counter-attraction. She swum from the old orbit to the new. Lord Rochester took her under his protection—whatever exactly that meant. Meanwhile the tales persisted. The Duchess removed her favourite from the companionship of the Maids to more immediate attendance on her person. Miss Bagot had also withdrawn; she had married, first, to Lady Castlemaine's annoyance, Charles Berkeley, Earl of Falmouth, and, after his death in battle, Charles Sackville, Earl of Dorset. This depletion of the Maids left two vacancies. Out of a number of candidates the Duchess, in order to fill them, chose Miss Frances Jennings and Miss Anne Temple.

Frances Jennings was the elder sister of a more celebrated lady, Sarah Jennings, whom she afterwards brought to Court, being thus the first instrument of the romantic love between Sarah and John Churchill. Afterwards, when both ladies were Duchesses—Sarah of Marlborough and the favourite of Queen Anne, Frances of Tyrconnel and a fugitive with the Old Pretender—they could not always sustain friendly relations. But as yet Sarah was at St. Albans and no one, and Frances was at Whitehall and very much someone. Exactly what kind of someone she would be she gave her attention to decide. With a just realism she determined " not to dispose of her heart until she gave her hand," and she left both in charge of her head. Until that acquiesced, Frances Jennings determined not to allow any part of her to be at the disposal of peer or prince. The Duke of York made advances; she dropped his notes along the galleries from the pockets into which they had been slipped. She became the admiration and the Duke the amusement of the Court. The King heard of it; ironically sceptical, he thought of testing Miss Jennings in the fire of royalty. But Miss Stewart, though she gave him nothing but smiles, made difficulties about his giving more than smiles elsewhere to Miss Jennings. Charles returned to her, to Lady Castlemaine, and to lesser social spoil. Miss Jennings, a Caroline and sophisticated Una, continued to advance safely through the artificial forest of the links and candles.

Anne Temple was less intelligent, less cool, and (to a degree) less fortunate. She was the daughter of a Warwickshire squire and of the daughter of a Surrey squire; the country had formed her. Almost like a young woman in one of the contemporary theatrical comedies, with fine teeth, fresh complexion, and an attractive smile, she came surprisingly to the Court. Her mouth was prepared to open and her eyes to languish; her heart was ready for vanity and her mind for credulity. She was extremely attractive and extremely silly.

Lord Rochester was nineteen, and had lost his first modesty. He had at the moment nothing to do. He had been engaged recently with a lady, and had received offence, in that connexion, from another of the Maids, a Miss Price. In revenge he had denigrated Miss Price in a copy of verses, by all reports devastatingly intimate, inaccurate, and obscene. But that done, he looked round the Court and observed the new arrivals. It appeared possible to him to derive entertainment from Anne Temple's physical advantages and mental disadvantages. He was becoming used to his power, and he enjoyed acting. He proceeded to act. Miss Temple saw him; she heard that this was the brilliant young lord, the master of satirical verse, of whom all the Court was in fear. He gazed; less wise than Miss Jennings, she gazed back.

Presently she discovered that the admiring gaze was fixed, not on her very pretty figure but on her mind. He was impervious, thus he confided in her, to all but intelligential charms. Had it been otherwise, she would undoubtedly have overcome him; as it was, he could enjoy " the most delightful interchange in the world " without any risks of baser excitements. In a passion of intellectual ardour, Miss Temple reciprocated. He produced his latest poems; she listened, commented, was enthralled. It was understood to be almost by accident that these poems so often celebrated Miss Temple's perfections. The subject, they both realized, was immaterial; it was the poetry with which they were concerned.

In fact, one must not too rashly blame the pretty foolishness of Anne Temple. Rochester's poems were quite capable of soaring into an intellectual air. Among those preserved to us is one at least which exhorts Chloris to higher things than pleasure:

> Then, Chloris, while I Duty pay,
>   The Nobler Tribute of my Heart,
> Be not You so severe to say
>   You love me for a frailer part.

Under what name, or if under any of those that remain to us—Chloris, Phyllis, Celia—he admired the polished corners of the Temple, we cannot tell. If he exhorted her to severity, it was poetry; if to union, it was still poetry.

The Duchess beheld the intellectual companionship and deplored it. Her new Maid's head was swimming with new wine. Yet to forbid Miss Temple to entertain Lord Rochester's Muse was as foolish and futile as to forbid her to entertain Lord Rochester. With the one she was wholly intimate; with the other, only partially. The Duchess did not see her way to interfere imperatively either with what was established or with what was perhaps unintended. She consulted and instructed Miss Hobart. Let Miss Hobart break up the conversations, show a friendship for Anne Temple, and intercept consequences which everyone but their victim expected, and perhaps, more than she well knew, even the victim herself. Miss Hobart, remembering the defection of Sarah Cooke, addressed herself, in a double sense, to the charge.

The delighted Court beheld the duel of opposite mysteries of sex. The prize was ignorant of the battle. She had naturally not been able, considering where she was, to avoid some rumour of the side of Lord Rochester's reputation which was not merely terror. She could not escape a suspicion—a not entirely disagreeable suspicion —that he was not quite as impervious to women's

THE DUEL WITH MISS HOBART

charms as he declared. Men, Miss Temple knew, were apt to be moved and thrilled, however pure their intellectual interests. She found Miss Hobart a phœnix of another colour. Miss Hobart could not possibly have designs, which neither, up to date, had Lord Rochester, or so he candidly said. Miss Hobart also said that Anne Temple was clever . . . and good . . . and beautiful. Also Miss Hobart had a cupboard of sweets and cordials. Miss Temple adored sweets and cordials.

It was summer. Miss Temple came in one day from riding, her mind running before her to the cupboard. She dismounted; she ran up to her friend's room; she looked in. Miss Hobart welcomed her with a charming freedom. Miss Temple, unwilling to go too far from the cupboard, asked if she might change her habit there. The small effort pokes up absurdly in that high diplomatic conflict of the Hobart and the Wilmot. But it was the sweets that Miss Temple wanted, and she took the obvious way to them. Miss Hobart immediately took the obvious way to what she wanted. She threw aside the dignity of her age and position; she begged to assist her friend. In a delightful harmony the disrobing began.

While it went on, Miss Hobart provided

another kind of sweetmeat—more like Lord Rochester's, but in prose. She spoke of the other recent Maid, Frances Jennings—how foolish, how sluttish, how painted, how dirty! how she only washed her face and hands! Miss Hobart, among her duties, superintended the Duchess's bathroom, which was indeed near at hand, with only a withdrawing-room between. The changing finished and the sweetmeats eaten, the two ladies, at Miss Hobart's suggestion, passed into the withdrawing-room. Opposite them, as they entered, was a glass partition dividing it from the baths proper; on the other side of it hung curtains of Chinese taffeta, now closely drawn. By the partition was a couch. The ladies disposed themselves affectionately upon it, and continued to talk; or rather, Miss Hobart continued to talk. Anne Temple, and one other, listened. Within the curtained bathroom, within the bath, indeed—a full bath of cold water— Sarah Cooke quivered and listened.

She had no business there. In the days when she and Miss Hobart had been friends, perhaps she might have been allowed the privilege. The privilege should have ended with the friendship, but Miss Hobart had a maid, and Sarah had prevailed upon the maid. Sarah too had a liking for cleanliness; also, she had an appointment with Lord Rochester that evening. The obliging maid had filled the bath with cold water —in the best English tradition. Most of the great old English traditions begin after the Restoration of Charles II.; those that do not mostly went out with the Revolution against his brother. Cold water apparently remained. Sarah got in. Suddenly and inconveniently, the great ladies had been heard near at hand. The maid pulled the taffeta curtains, fled, and locked the bathroom door behind her; there was no time and no way for Sarah to escape. She remained, a mortgage of cleanliness, and presently the voices of the ladies percolated through the partition, and heated the heart in her uncommonly chilled body.

She heard Miss Hobart lamenting the bestial nature of men, with more emotion than Hobbes had commented on the base nature of mankind. The life of love in men seemed to her, as the life of man in nature seemed to Hobbes, " poor, nasty, brutish, and short," and only not " solitary," because solitude was impossible to its fulfilment. But solitary in the sense of egocentric Miss Hobart thought it, nor indeed was she far wrong, for without the operation of the will and the intellect, without the discovery of a strange spiritual Leviathan of *caritas*, "nasty, brutish, and short" it seems usually to be. The lady, however, did not diverge into such philosophical problems. She deprecated marriage, which has been attempted as one method of solution, and offered no other, except a general despite, towards which she proposed practical examples; remarking on the various gentlemen who professed to admire Miss Temple —Henry Sidney, "handsome but a fool"; Charles Lyttelton, honest and boorish; Lord Rochester—ah, Lord Rochester! "Wittiest and most dishonourable of men," he desired to ensnare for the mere sake of ensnaring; where he could not possess in action, he would possess in poetry; persuasive, hypocritical, ruffianly, malign, potent through his wit to conquer, impotent through his debauches to enjoy; the terror of well-born Maids, and the favourite of common prostitutes. He set out to ensnare, but where he ensnared he could give and take no delight in his spoil.

Anne Temple had no intention of being snared, but it was tiresome to think that the result of the snare, had it succeeded, would have been as cerebral as the snare itself. She was given no time to meditate; Miss Hobart was passing to another topic. This man, this abomination of intellect, grace, and bestiality, addresses

himself to Miss Temple that he may give an
appearance of actuality to the calumnious fictions
he breathes out concerning her! Anne stared;
the fictions Lord Rochester had shown her were
of quite another kind. " You look as if you
didn't believe me," Miss Hobart exclaimed—
truthfully; "you needn't rely on my word!
Look here! Here's evidence for you "—she pulled
a paper from her pocket—" look what kind of
verses he is writing about you while he is carrying
on his deceptions."

Anne looked at the paper. Incredible—but
true! There the dreadful couplets were, extravagantly destructive, extravagantly obscene. She
was libelled and ridiculed, in person and mind.
Her very name flared at her. Miss Hobart began
to hum the lines. Anne, her folly outraged, her
credulity betrayed, something that had not yet
become expectation mocked and defeated, burst
into hysterical anger. She wept in misery; she
cried out that she wasn't like that—she might
not be as beautiful as some people, but she wasn't
like *that*—she wasn't—her friend could see—
they were alone—and . . . and she had a good
mind to show . . . the poor country girl raged on.

So far they did not go. The Hobart com-
forted, consoled, cosseted, advised silence and
scorn. Let Anne avoid Rochester; his lies,

after all, were too notorious for these to be believed. She restored her friend to anguished calm. Together they rose; they passed out of the withdrawing-room. The maid, as soon as she could, slipped back, and young Sarah, at last coming out of the bath, fled away to make her preparations for the coming of the terrible Earl. Her limbs were chilly, but her heart was burning. She repeated to herself, as she went, as she moved about, the slanders Miss Hobart had uttered. She had her own troubles, and at the moment the greatest of these was undoubtedly Anne Temple.

Rochester came. Sarah poured out the story. Even the young Earl's admirable presence of mind was a little taken aback. He remembered the song well enough; it was the one he had made on Goditha Price. He admired the dexterity with which Miss Hobart had manipulated the words in order to substitute Temple for Price. He recognized her adequate vengeance, but he did not propose to allow her to escape so—nor, for that matter, Miss Temple. John Wilmot did not propose to be defeated by a—by Miss Hobart. Sarah began to inquire about Miss Temple; was it true that he——? He smiled back at her. "Can you doubt it," he asked, "since that paragon of sincerity affirms it? But don't worry; it is obvious my treachery will do me no good, since my own debauchery and the London prostitutes have brought me to order, whether I like it or not!" He consoled Sarah; then, the pleasant hour ended, he went, still bent on a bright revenge. The Duchess held court that evening. Lord Rochester determined to go. Sarah was left to her attic, but under the candles the rest of them met.

The two ladies came together. The Lord Rochester was a little late. Miss Hobart's hand lay on Miss Temple's arm, not wholly from Lesbian affection. Miss Hobart had, in fact, started not so much a hare as a fox, and a fox with a torch tied to its tail. The anger in Anne's heart could not be subdued, neither by natural grace nor by courtly habit. To the easy insincerities of the gay company she tittered awkward sincerities of indignation. The verses were known, she supposed, to the whole Court, as most of their author's were. She, and only she, had hitherto been unaware; she would show all of them that she now knew. Miss Hobart might nudge; Miss Hobart might pinch; nothing checked her. She had never been so pretty as now, on fire with shame. People gathered round her; the lords and gentlemen offered courtesies. She replied with a bitterness that seared her own heart to compliments on her brilliant colour or her sparkling eyes. "Oh, everyone knows I'm almost a monster . . . all is not gold that glitters . . . company-compliments mean nothing . . . in fact, I'm a mere fright." Her heart was hot; she spake with her tongue. The Court, amazed and amused, watched the public kindling of the secret flame. Eyebrows lifted; voices murmured. Miss Temple was a figure. In the midst of the melodious turmoil my lord Rochester arrived.

More debonair than she in irony, he approached. She saw him, and for a moment burned more brilliantly red. Then, as her agitation grew on her, she paled, impetuously stepped forward, stepped back, pulled on her gloves, violently manœuvred with her fan. Miss Hobart's grasp was firm. The young man came up, surveying them both. Anne Temple turned half away. He smiled; she saw it, and threw herself farther from that insult of laughter. More adept in courtly movement than the still untransformed country girl, he was agile to face her. Eyes to eyes he met her; the Hobart he ignored. "Indeed, madam, nothing can be a greater tribute to you than to shine as you do to-night, after so tiring a day. To bear a three hours' ride, and Miss Hobart afterwards, and not to be utterly exhausted—that is a triumph of natural vigour, indeed!"

The full ambiguity was lost on Anne, but she did not need to know it. It was too much that the loathed slanderer should dare to address her. Her eyes blazed at him. Miss Hobart, in extreme alarm, pinched her furiously. Before the choking Maid could break into the uncourtly abuse she desired, the smiling Earl made her a courtesy of farewell, and lightly moved away.

It was but a temporary withdrawal. He proposed a more entire victory, and he set his secret agents to work. Miss Hobart found young Sarah making timid approaches, trying to be friendly. She too, it seemed, was abandoning Lord Rochester. It is to be feared Miss Hobart began to suffer from *hubris*; that or mere inefficiency of intrigue blinded her to the danger of such offered amity. Lord Rochester had conferred with Sarah's aunt, the Mother of the Maids; by their instructions Sarah was sent to the Hobart, to their ears she repeated everything she heard. The Hobart, alarmed at the public defiance which the Earl had offered her, and at his supposed knowledge of her secret talk, blamed her maid for treachery, and dismissed her. This was the result of the only act of simple goodwill in the whole business—the poor creature's good-natured introduction of Sarah into the Duchess's bath. There was a new maid, who (it is gratifying to learn) ate the sweets which had been the fatal lure. Sarah, more familiar and useful to the Hobart through this change, heard more and repeated all. Presently she came back to her superiors with something worth hearing.

The shell that had exploded through Anne Temple's spirit had fired her temper, and now she was not easily controlled. The Court had a habit, and sometimes a mania, for masks and disguises. Anne took it into her head that she also would walk disguised one evening in the Mall. She proposed the scheme to her friend; they would change dresses, they would wear vizards and scarves. Miss Hobart objected; her objections were overwhelmed. Somehow Anne was determined to speak to Rochester, to unload her stuffed bosom, to reproach, to devastate, to annihilate him. If she could not do it in her own person, she could in the form of another. Miss Hobart, not quite understanding this intention, but generally apprehensive, was compelled to submit.

Rochester, hearing all this, or hearing some and guessing more, sent for a friend, Henry Killigrew, and taught him his part in this scene of the comedy. It was almost absurdly close to the Caroline stage; the Park by chance that evening almost deserted; the straight line of the Mall; the two ladies scarved, masked, disguised, moving along it; the two gentlemen, superbly themselves, advancing in the distance towards them. Anne knew them—at least she knew Rochester. She quickened her steps. Miss Hobart sought delay, murmuring remonstrances. " Surely . . . surely . . . those two devils . . . exposed to their insolence . . ." It was useless. " At least don't talk with him." Anne promised she would not answer Rochester; she promised anything. As the unreliable vow was uttered, the gentlemen came up. Rochester sprang to the apparent Miss Temple's side; Killigrew attached himself to the real Miss Temple. Anne was furious; Miss Hobart was delighted. The intentions of two of them, and the willingness of the third, defeated the passion of the fourth. The two pairs drew apart. Killigrew lost no time. " Ah, Miss Hobart, this is a lucky chance. I have been wanting to speak to you. You know I'm your servant and friend; I want to warn you."

Anne, her curiosity roused, paused where she was. " In God's name, why must you attack Lord Rochester in the way you do ? " Killigrew's voice thrilled in her ear. "You know quite well he is one of the most honourable men in the Court, yet you continually slander him as a scoundrel to the very person he holds in the highest respect . . ." The voice thrilled on. Killigrew poured out his speech. He exclaimed and rebuked, remonstrated and exhorted. Through shocked sentences of mingled surprise and admonition, Lord Rochester began to appear as an angel of light, and his feminine rival to take on darker and darker shades. Anne Temple heard herself, as Miss Hobart, defined in hints of unimaginable monstrosity. She became Lesbian, lewd, hermaphroditic; women were ruined and children born by her. The swords of the gentlemen she had slandered gleamed threateningly round her; especially the stoical figure of Sir Charles Lyttelton, who loomed barbaric in a desperate purpose of revenge. Among those offended figures appeared the beautiful spirits of Anne Temple and John Wilmot. The dreadful verses were not about *her*; they were about Goditha Price, who had no doubt deserved them. Sir Charles Lyttelton was passionate; Lord Rochester was pure. Everything in the Mall was lovely, except only the venomous web-spinning spider of a Hobart whom Mr. Killigrew, of course, conceived himself to be rebuking.

"The Angel ended." Rochester and his companion reappeared.

Anne had no time or tongue for more. As soon as, with mutual salutations, the ladies and gentlemen had parted, she turned back to the palace. Dazed with delight and horror, she hurried along, the newly revealed monstrosity scurrying by her side. The monstrosity spoke sometimes, but Anne did not heed. She desired only to get away. Confusion worse-confounded resolved itself in her into two purposes—to be done with Miss Hobart, and to be begun again, as soon as possible, with the injured and innocent Rochester. She rushed to her own room; she tore off the borrowed gown, the clothing of that malign double-sexed horror, whose maid had given birth, whose corrupt caresses had even touched herself. She thrust the gown at her own maid, bidding her take it back at once, and recover her own. That done, she felt a little easier, and proceeded more slowly with the rest of her toilet. All would yet be well. She had trusted an animal and been deceived in a saint. Lord Rochester was a man of honour; Sir Charles Lyttelton was a man of controlled passion. The one admired her—did she sigh? The other loved her—did she smile? In a firm resolution of having no more to do with Miss Hobart, of even forgoing the sweets and cordials, she proceeded symbolically to change her linen; in the midst of which freshening and significant business she suddenly felt Miss Hobart's arm about her, heard Miss Hobart's voice in her ear, and saw Miss Hobart's "satyr eyes" leering at her face.

That poor deceived lady had not been able to make out what had happened. Rochester, thinking, as she supposed he supposed, that he was talking to Miss Temple, had been civil but not very forthcoming. But what had Killigrew said — what could Killigrew say — to Anne? Questions panted during their swift return had gone unanswered. And then the dress, so suddenly, so violently, returned, with that imperious demand for her own. Something mischievous must have intruded. She told the maid to stay where she was, and herself went off to Anne's lodging. In she slipped, saw Anne changing, determined to be affectionate first and inquisitive afterwards, approached silently, and threw her arm round the meditative Maid.

Anne shrieked, and went on shrieking. She felt herself clutched by a horror, and could not guess what outrage might be worked on her. She screamed to God; she screamed to her friends. It was close on midnight when those cries rang wildly down the gallery. People came running—the maids and the Maids and the Mother of the Maids. Sarah came. They poured in; they saw Miss Temple warding off Miss Hobart, and Miss Hobart trying to get at Miss Temple. The Mother, sailing in, broke into exclamations. Virtuous and victorious, she denounced the foulness that broke by night into the rooms of the Duchess's Maids. At last, Miss Hobart, distracted by what seemed to her a universal lunacy, fled. The sympathy of the Maids enveloped Miss Temple for the night, and the next morning Sarah related to the Earl of Rochester the spectacular rout of his enemy.

The victory would have been even more complete had it not been for the action of royalty. The jests and tales of the Court concerning Miss Hobart seemed now justified. In the Court and beyond the Court—in that London society which battened on the Court—she had lost all human reputation. Only one person—foolishly, selfishly, or honourably—stood by her, and that was the Duchess of York. The Court whispered that the Duchess had private reasons for supporting Miss Hobart, but they whispered in private. In public her support was effectual. She scorned the wild fable, and she acted. Miss Temple was sent for, and severely scolded for her credulity.

The Mother of the Maids was dismissed for deliberate falsehood, and Sarah went with her. The Maids in general were rebuked.

The Duchess had scolded, but not as harshly as Anne now scolded herself. She had rashly believed the Hobart; now, as rashly, she believed Killigrew. She longed to be Rochester's friend once more, to abase herself, to make any kind of reparation. He was the noblest man and the greatest genius of his kind and time. She yearned for him; unfortunately, Rochester's more purely intellectual activities intervened. When Anne, in the course of a few days, began to seek for him, she found that the momentary anger of the King at some rasher insult than usual had intervened. The Earl had been forbidden the Court, and had retired into the country.[1] Sir Charles Lyttelton, however, remained. Presently, before the end of May 1666, Anne married him. He was a much more reliable person than John Wilmot, Earl of Rochester; she bore him thirteen children. She never again had the chance of being teased, flattered, admired, and insulted by genius. And since we owe all

[1] So Hamilton. But it was early days for banishments. Could we assume that he had departed on his second naval expedition, or to the country to make preparations for it, it would be simpler. It would leave him more reasonably placed with Miss Mallet on his return.

we know of the episode to Anthony Hamilton, and since Anthony Hamilton always put the fastidiously worst construction on everything, and since Lord Rochester was both a romantic and a poet, it is to this day impossible to know whether indeed that single interlude was a mere scene in the opening search for sensation, or whether it were rather one of the moments in which the impatient imagination which is an exaltation rather than a decay of sense occupied itself in discovering intellectual delight ; whether indeed he desired, as he said, poetry rather than love.

CHAPTER V

THE DUEL WITH LORD MULGRAVE

" —SOE greate a disproportion 'twixt our desires and what is ordained to content them . . ."

It is the beginning of an undated fragment of a letter from the Earl of Rochester to his Countess. The Countess indeed may have thought so. She lived in the country, visited sometimes by her lord, sometimes by the Dowager Countess, with whom she had difficulties. The disproportion in her life, if she felt it, was definite and flagrant. In her husband's it was concealed, but no less present.

The Earl had returned finally to the Court. His desires had been discontented, in the matter of death and supernatural visitation, with what was ordained. The smaller universe of Charles Stuart was to prove no more satisfactory in what it ordained than the larger universe of God Almighty. It is not at best easy to unite the world of intellect and the world of sensation; only perhaps in great art can they both be experienced at once. The movements of the flesh and of the mind pass along separated channels; philosophy can make roads by which we can pass to the banks of either great stream, but even philosophy itself can rarely dig canals along which the waters of both may mingle. Yet, separate, they can hardly be justified. My lord desired to give his mind sensations which could be justified, and his body an intellect which could approve it. It was an effort with which the world of the King's grandfather, James I., and his contemporaries had been thoroughly familiar—that and the world of the Elizabethan generation immediately preceding. Then the poets, the preachers, and even the politicians had felt the double claim of mind and body, and one way or another had invented, by exploration or craft, a satisfaction. The appearance of Elizabeth or James had appeased sensation by the person of the Monarch while the theory of divine viceroyalty had fed the intellect. The royal progresses and pageants had displayed the spectacle of incarnate government. The theatre had achieved, for some few years, a similar unity. From Marlowe to Webster intellect dealt physical shocks at the audience—shocks that were no less marvels of double intellectual and physical composition because few perhaps of the varied audience immediately recognized them as such. The metaphysical poets had carried on the tradition, though they increased the proportion of intellect, and sometimes added another and lower element—ingenuity. Their passion composed itself in the twisted dance of verbal meanings. But still the sensations they bestowed were shocks, vigorous shocks, of delight. Rather eloquent than pure their blood spoke in their verses, and so divinely wrought that one might almost say their bodies thought. The sermons did not lose the habit. Before the King's father, Charles, in 1631, Donne preached his last sermon, and battered his hearers with the resonant latinities into which he had translated his awareness of death. Indeed, death itself was eloquent; scaffolds were tortuous with pulsing epigrams and orations. Whatever divisions of controversy existed under Elizabeth and James, this at least was common to all disputants—a power of prose and verse that often arose from an almost conscious aspiration after unity of mind and body, so that they discovered in their speech an instrument of unity, and wildness and restraint lived together in their world.

That world changed. The poet whom Rochester greatly admired was not Donne, but Cowley. Cowley, though he was of the breed, was a younger son, and at that seems sometimes disinherited of the metaphysical laurel. He could not be physically dominant; even his best verse is at one remove from the body, and even his admirer recognized it. "Not being of God, he could not stand," the poet in Rochester commented. The King whom Rochester served was not James I. but Charles II. Those two Kings had much in common; they were the most intelligent of the later Stuarts. But Charles never attempted to thrust on his courtiers or his people the strange esoteric doctrine of the corporeal royalty in which James was so ardent a believer. He sought to maintain a subdued theory of monarchy, but he also made his person easy. Elizabeth had been popular, but she had always been able to shroud herself in the glory of her sacred identity with her office. James, less competently, had tried to carry on the tradition. Charles, in effect, brought the monarchy down into the world. He had no choice, for he and his world no longer walked in the dark spiritual forest. The Park was less tolerant of mystical visions of the Crown; there such things would have been slightly absurd—as ungentlemanly as for a husband who was a gentleman to be jealous of his wife. Monarchy and monogamy had lost their romanticism.

"Imagination is nothing else than decaying

sense." Sense in the physical energy and "decaying sense" in the mental comment were divided. The division affected all things, and love among them. Attention was directed rather to the sense than to the "decaying sense," and imagination deserted the love affairs of the Court. They lost intellect; they became sensational. But no activity of man can wholly lose intellect, and what intellect remained had therefore to devote itself to the sensation. What is the chief quality of a sensation? It is temporary, it is a "flying moment." To the "flying moment," in its failure or success, the thoughts, fancies, and poems of the civilized man were therefore now directed. To that the philosophy of Hobbes and the taste of Charles both assisted it.

There were at the time two courts, the royal court of Charles and the ducal court of his brother James. Both of those princes were men of high culture. Both of them had a genuine apprehension of the forest of man's dreams and desires—such a forest as, not so long before, Milton had exhibited in *Comus*. Both of them had a very real desire for the utmost possible tolerance of the visions and prophecies seen and heard in it. George Fox and his new Society of Friends were able to invoke the goodwill of the King. Both King and Duke were aware also of the two great high-roads which had been driven through the aboriginal wood, and neither of them were, by this time, disposed to follow that which lay under the jurisdiction of Canterbury. But there the likeness stopped. The King concealed his emotions and his judgment. The Duke admitted his. Both of them exposed their sensations.

The King's sensations had for long been connected with Barbara Villiers, Lady Castlemaine, who had, after the Restoration, allowed her own to be aroused. A characteristic of those flying sensations is that they usually need fresh excitements. In 1663 the King had compelled Lady Castlemaine to admit the Lady Frances Stewart, Mistress Mallet's friend, to her suppers. He had, on the other hand, never succeeded in compelling or persuading the guest to admit him, after the suppers, to her more intimate favours. Even the adoption of her face for that of Britannia on the coinage did not seduce her from her resolution. As if in a passion of care for the public morality of succeeding generations she remained virtuous. In 1667, the year of Rochester's return, she married the Duke of Richmond, much to the King's anger. At the same time Lady Castlemaine, like the Dutch and the House of Commons, was being tiresome.

Peace had been made with the Dutch. But of the lady it was said—and might have been said of the House of Commons—" How imperious this woman is, and hectors the King to whatever she will." The battle between them moved from subject to subject. In the month of the Dutch peace, it turned on whether the child which Lady Castlemaine was carrying was the King's, or (more exactly) whether the King should agree that it was. Neither of them was in a position to quarrel over the right of paternity. Charles was occupied not only with the unprocurable Frances Stewart, but with the more complaisant actress, Moll Davies. Lady Castlemaine had been attracted by Henry Jermyn, a little fat man, of a recurrence in the Court affairs of the time. He was said to be about to marry Lady Falmouth. Lady Castlemaine's anger broke out. The King's intelligence did not apparently save him from jealousy. "The King is mad at her entertaining Jermyn, and she is mad at Jermyn's going to marry from her, so they are all mad and thus the kingdom is governed!" wrote Pepys, on 29th July 1667. The moral reflection was unworthy of him. Sensations do not necessarily interfere with the executive intelligence.

The turmoil in the ducal court of James was

less noisy, though His Highness was not far behind his brother in regard to the interest he took in the ladies of his Court. The Maids of Honour of the Duchess were the contemplation of the heir-presumptive, as the Queen's Maids were of the King. But James had not his brother's gifts of procrastination in other things. Charles, safeguarding his emotions from others, perhaps safeguarded some of his intellectual decisions even from himself. No one knows at what moment, if at all, before his submission on his death-bed, he determined that his religious obedience was properly due to the Roman See. The moment—or at least the year or so—when James made a similar decision is flagrant. It was between 1669 and 1671. The easy smiles of the world have encouraged us to believe that a firm, unpopular, and even dangerous intellectual adherence to a Creed is incompatible with infidelities in action to the morals of that Creed, but in fact (as we all very well know) it is not so. Both before and after his conversion the Duke was spasmodically concerned with his wife's ladies. On one occasion Gilbert Burnet " took the freedom to object to him . . . that the rest of his life was not so exact," that his religious zeal could be believed to flow from an inward sense of his duty to God—otherwise, it would appear in other things. This is always the objection it is so easy to make to other people's behaviour: if they were sincere in one thing, they would of course be sincere in all. The Duke answered with a sentence of extraordinary and humble nobility. He said " that a man might have a persuasion of his duty to God so as to restrain him from dissembling with God and men in professing himself to be of another religion than that which he believed was true, though it did not yet restrain all his appetites." Let us be fair to Burnet; it was he who recorded both question and answer. And James, to be fair to him in turn, seems to have confined himself to the simplest appetite. One of the ladies said afterwards, of the ducal mistresses, "What he saw in any of us I cannot tell. We were all plain, and if any of us had had wit, he would not have understood it."

This limited nature of James's mind, however, was not very closely akin to Rochester's, and there is nothing to show that the Earl's exploring intellect found it at all suggestive that both the Duchess and the Duke of York persisted, to their own serious disadvantage, in following the Roman way through the forest. He wrote a lampoon on the Duke's conversion, in which he attributed it not to logic but to the grace of God.

What he said in the character of the Duke, in lines not uncharacteristic of himself, was :

> Father Patrick, I find,
> By the sudden Conversion, and Change of my Mind,
> It is not your Reason, nor Wit, can afford
> Such Strength to your Cause ; 'tis the Finger o' th' Lord :
> For now I remember, he some where has said,
> That by Babes and by Sucklings his Truth is Convey'd.

It was mockery, and any foolish courtier might have written it. But it was Rochester, though in mockery, who did write it, and it was Rochester who desired " extraordinary impulses," and if religion, then the Finger of the Lord, and the extreme romanticism of religion.

He belonged, however, rather to the royal court than the ducal. Among the many conversations which the King held with his young servant, the subject of the nature of salvation probably did not in any seriousness arise. Nor were there any others, except the official clergy of both Churches, who were likely to discuss it. The two royal brothers were, in fact, least likely of all to follow in their inmost hearts " the flying moment." They had intellect ; they had culture ; they had conscience. But Charles, against a background of longer time, half in actuality, half in dissimulation, collected as many fugitive sensations as he could, and James could not yet prevent himself appetitively watching for them. There was, however, one supreme devotee of the god who had appeared at the nativity of John Wilmot—Mercury, the god of speed and passage; one master of hasty conversions and swift changes of mind: it was George Villiers, second Duke of Buckingham.

He was the son of the Favourite of James I., and he possessed all his father's disadvantages with none of his capacity. History, which so often justifies the poets, has justified Dryden's portrait of Buckingham—

> Who in the course of one revolving moon
> Was chemist, fiddler, statesman, and buffoon.

To add traitor might be too violent, but at least he deserted every cause, and always the King's. He had made friends with Cromwell; he supported the ridiculous gasconades of Monmouth. Of him might be said what Clarendon wrote of the Lord Jermyn, that he "who in his own judgement was very indifferent in all matters relating to religion, was always of some faction that regarded it." He made inconsistency spectacular; his desertions and disloyalties were flagrant, as flagrant as the deaths that sometimes accompanied them. Few figures, even in that age, were so wildly related to such extreme

DUEL WITH LORD MULGRAVE 91

opposites. He fell in love with and "seduced" the Countess of Shrewsbury; he killed the husband in a duel. That was in 1668; in 1670, during a diplomatic mission to Paris, the French King presented him with ten thousand livres for the lady. By 1674 he had become "the apostle of Protestantism and Patriotism," was denouncing his fellow-diplomat, Arlington, in the Lords, and was promising that august body on his own behalf and the Countess's that they would cease cohabitation. By 1678 he was one of the makers and leaders of the Plot that was only too dreadfully not Popish. Yet all this while he had remained one of the King's friends. Early in 1677 he had been sent to the Tower by the Lords for declaring that Parliament had been automatically dissolved. In August, Andrew Marvell wrote to a friend:

"The D: of Buckingham petitiond only that he had layd so long, had contracted severall indispositions and desired a moneths aire. This was by Nelly, Midlesex, Rochester, and the merry gang easily procured with presumption to make it an intire liberty. Hereupon he layd constantly in Whitehall at my L: Rochester's logings leading the usuall life. The D: of Yorke, the Treasurer and, they tell me too, the D: of

Munmoth, remonstrated to the King that this was to leap over all rules of decency and to suffer his authority to be trampled on but if he had a fauor for him he might do it in a regular way etc. Neverthelesse it was for some days a moot point betwixt the Ministers of State and Ministers of Pleasure who should carry it. At last Buck. was advertised that he should retire out of Whitehall. He obeyd and since presented they say a more acknowledging Petition then either Salisburyes or Wharton's whereupon I heare that he was yesterday by the same Rule dismissed. People were full of vaine imaginations what changes he would make in Court but he loves Pleasure better than Revenge and yet this last is not the meanest luxury."

Buckingham is, in fact, a point from which one can discern two things—the two extremes of Hobbes and Fox, or rather the two chaotic parodies which attended the extremes of Hobbes and Fox. Two beasts, which might better be called boar and mule than leviathan and lamb appear together, and the mischievous childishness of Buckingham for a moment leads them. One is the dark underlying power of outbreak in common men—Anabaptistry, Fifth Monarchism, Bolshevism. The other is the obstinate selfishness of the cultured man. Death, in those days, attended on both. There was a very real awareness of the danger of a bloody revolt by the Saints. In the first year of Charles's reign there was such an outbreak in London, when armed men shouting " King Jesus ! " ran through the streets, killing whom they met, and the fear of such attack lasted. In 1671 a cow got loose and ran towards Westminster Hall, causing a mild tumult. Swords were drawn, staffs caught up, and among those who at a distance could not see the cow a cry arose that the Fifth Monarchy men were out and coming to cut the throats of the lawyers. It was partly such fears that caused the distrust of all " enthusiasm."

On the other hand, the unenthusiastic aristocracy maintained their own peculiar privilege of murder. Duels were the least unjust method ; mere killing was not infrequent. The Lord Cornwallis struck down a footboy in St. James's Park ; Mr. Floyd stabbed a cook in a tavern. The Lord Rochester was mixed up with a killing at Epsom. There was a callous casualness about the swords of the gentry, which had not even the excuse of the romantic vision of King Jesus or the pretence of a serious loyalty to King Charles. Even the Court ladies were concerned. In 1683 the Lady Mary Gerrard and some others had a frolic. They put on masculine dress, and walked the streets with some gentlemen. "In Leicester fields they mett wth a fidler, and I know n^{t} on what provocations, but ye poore man was killed amongst them, 'tis said they are in ye Gate House"—so the Verney letters. "The flying moment" was enough, for murder as for love, and its wings were immediate sensational profit and loss. It had no sufficiency, nor desired it; it hurried to give way to the next.

To this Court, ruled by Charles, whose extreme was Buckingham, Rochester, the spiritual child of Donne and the first Buckingham, returned. He shone in it as a star, but a star which was something of a portent. He was "wild." There were, at that time, two kinds of wildness. The first, which was unfashionable, was a wild devotion to some supernatural or semi-supernatural cause; that was *enthusiasm*. The second, which was not unfashionable, was a wild behaviour in natural things; that was *extravagance*. No one accused Rochester of the first; he denied it himself. "I was never an enthusiast." Directed enthusiasm was what he desired and needed, but could not find. Undirected enthusiasm ran wild into extravagance. He was not alone in that, at such a Court; it is the more to be noted that he was notable in it. "Extravagant mirth," "pleasing extravagance," "riotous extravagance," wrote Gilbert Burnet, Rochester's French biographer, and Anthony Wood respectively. Excess entered into what he did, what he said, and what he wrote ; an excess which had in its heat something of genius, and in its habit a literal intoxication. In one of his poems he called poetry " a stormy pathless world." He was right, but few others in that age would have conceived or used such a phrase. He plunged, as stormily as his own world permitted, into the only world he could find, and along its candle-bright paths. He was, said Anthony Wood, " for some years in one almost uninterrupted fit of Wantonness and Intemperance." Rochester put it more shortly to Burnet, when he said that for five years together he was continually drunk.

He was certainly drunk with the desire of a greater intoxication ; that is, a spiritual. There moved in him an increasing contempt for his world, and the modesty of his first appearance was no longer observed. His mind was wild, for it ran level with his unformulated desire ; and in the end it was permitted to win the race. Imagination, those young poets had been taught, is nothing else but decaying sense. Rochester at least was preserved from that dreadful time when the failing senses attempt vainly to live up to that vapour of their decay, when life yearns after sensations it recollects and cannot compass. In the last year of those that remained his energy was to outrun his grisly competitor, and in the last three months of his race he passed triumphantly into the grave, Rochester still, and an intellectual victor over death and decay.

In his ambiguous position of a thing at once admired and feared, satire was his instrument. It is one of the most notorious facts about him that he did not confine his satire to his equals; he attacked with it his single great superior. He wrote at times bitter, and—to our tastes—filthy, sarcasms on Charles Stuart. He was repeatedly banished from Court on account of them. He made free with the King's mistresses in his verse, and exercised a certain freedom towards them in his behaviour. Barbara Villiers had become a Duchess. After a period of storm a kind of agreement between her and the King eased and in effect concluded their relations, about the same time as the more famous Treaty of Dover. She abandoned her hostility to the other ladies of the King's favour, limited her own favours in certain directions, and received the desired dignity. At some time after this had been conferred (3rd August 1670) the Duchess had driven out one day in her coach. She returned;

the coach stopped at the gate of Whitehall. Rochester happened to be by. He saw the Duchess alighting. He sprang forward—before the eyes of the public he made a motion to kiss her. The indignant Duchess—her sense of social, if not of personal, dignity aroused—struck at him with her fist. Rochester slipped and fell. He rose undismayed; undismayed, he cried out before them all :

> "By Heaven! 'twas bravely done.
> First, to attempt the Chariot of the Sun,
> And then to fall like Phaeton."

In general, however, he was not so gracefully complimentary. In a set of verses entitled *Lais Senior* he praised her as the greatest of prostitutes, comparing her omnipotent desires with those of famous ladies of antiquity. "Eclips'd," he ended, almost as Crashaw might have ended a passionate ode on a saint, with the very throb and movement of a metaphysical :

> Eclips'd by her, shall all forgotten be ;
> While her great Name confronts Eternity.

Nor did he confine his verse to the Duchess, whose power with the King might perhaps be supposed to be past. Louise Keroualle, Nell Gwynn, the Duchess Mazarin, Moll Davies, all had their share, and, repeatedly, the King. How many of the lines that mocked him, and mocked him with real ingenuity and wit, came to the King's eyes, we cannot tell. There is a story that Charles himself once drew a paper from Rochester's pocket, and found it to begin :

> Preserv'd by wonder in the Oak O C——s
> And then brought in by the Duke of Albemarle
> The first by Providence, the next all Devil,
> Show's thou'rt a Compound of Good and Evil—
> The Bad we'ave known too long, the Good's to come,
> But not expected till the Day of Doom ;
> Was ever Prince's Soul so meanly Poor
> To be a slave to—

after which, by means of the expected rhyme, it went off into more intimate obscenities. It was the cause of one of my lord's banishments ; it is said that from 1669 onwards they occurred regularly once a year. He was always recalled. He feared for his favour sometimes ; in 1673 his mother had been concerned in promoting a marriage that displeased the King. My Lord Rochester was reported to curse her and the young lady and all that made the match, " believing it will slaken the King's kindness to him." His fear was unnecessary, and as for the poems, the King was graciously pleased to regard them as " natural sallies of his genius," " meant as Sports of Fancy more than the Efforts of Malice." There was even more to it than that. " The King loved his company for the Diversion it afforded him." The King's own mind had a sense of proportion, and however far he yielded to his sensations he never overvalued them. He was indeed more just than Rochester, for he never overvalued his emotions nor expected the universe to answer their needs. Yet, alike in Charles Stuart's realism and in Rochester's romanticism, there was a sense of the universe. Their diversions could share a common mocking intelligence with something real in it, contradicting themselves, which their companions had not. The tale of the most famous of Rochester's epigrams holds them together. His Majesty (so report ran) said one day—it is the kind of thing Charles might have said on many days—that " he would leave every one to his liberty in talking . . . and would not take what was said at all amiss." The conversation touched on epitaphs. Rochester provided the King's :

> Here lies a great and mighty King
> Whose Promise none relies on ;
> He never said a foolish thing
> Nor ever did a wise one.

The King answered : " That is easily accounted for : my words are my own ; my actions are my ministers'." [1]

[1] So, at least, one tale. But it makes a very constitutional monarch of the Stuart.

The temper which was intellectually violent towards the King was sometimes physically violent towards social inferiors, and as the King was tolerant of the one so he was tolerant of the other. It is not given to every man to be careless of insults to himself and careful of injuries to his servants; it was not given to Charles. The Killigrews were a family of hangers-on of the Court. Sir Thomas Killigrew, who had spread among the Venetians the premature story of the victory at Worcester, and the still wilder story of the tendencious Puritan translation of the Koran, had been a friend of Henrietta Maria, Charles's mother. He had written idealistic plays for his prettily idealistic mistress, and afterwards a vulgar play for other tastes. He was, unfortunately, romantic too late for fashionable glory, and realistic too early for fashionable riches, and he was not very good at either kind of work. His sister had, for a brief while, been the King's mistress. His brother was the King's chaplain, and the Master of the Savoy, a post which he gained to the exclusion of Abraham Cowley, then out of favour because of his support of the Lord Protector. The chaplain's daughter, dying young, was immortalized by Dryden in his ode on Mistress Anne Killigrew. Sir Thomas's own son, Henry, who made himself of no reputation, was distinguished by the spasmodic companionship of Rochester. Sir Thomas himself was patentee and manager of the Theatre Royal in Drury Lane and the King's Company of actors. It was from this theatre, some years earlier, that Nell Gwynn had taken her degrees—bachelor of arts as an actress, master of arts as the King's mistress. Sir Thomas was therefore an old loyalist, well-meaning, rather inefficient, and heartily admonitory of others, especially of the King. He made no great success of his own affairs, but with a slightly excessive goodwill he rebuked the King for neglecting the kingdom's. The King took no notice ; in fact, he neglected them less than Killigrew supposed. Charles habitually made something of a spectacle of his sensations, but behind the spectacle he arrayed his powers for a serious political contest. Mr. Pepys heard from Mr. Pierce, who heard from Mr. Cowley, who heard with his own ears, how Sir Thomas had said to the King : " There is a good, honest, able man that I could name, that if your Majesty would employ, and give command to see all things well executed, all things would soon be mended ; and this is one Charles Stuart, who now spends his time employing his lips about the Court, and hath no other employment." " This, he says," Pepys wrote on—meaning Mr. Pierce—" is most true ; but the King do not profit by any of this, but lays all aside and remembers nothing, but to his pleasures again, which is a sorrowful consideration." A happy dispensation of Providence caused him, after this moral distress, to proceed "to the King's Playhouse . . . and the women do very well ; but above all little Nelly . . . the woman doing better than ever I expected, and very fine women."

This was on 8th December 1666, a day when Pepys had seen "smoke in the ruines" of London. It was two years later, on 16th February 1669, that Rochester and Sir Thomas came to a clash. The King with his suite had dined at the Dutch ambassador's. Among the courtiers were both Rochester and Killigrew. During the drinking and the raillery after dinner Killigrew, in his bluff good-tempered way, made a joke that was offensive to Rochester. Rochester, in a heat of wine, anger, nobility, and youth (he was twenty-one), struck him. Pepys, and people like Pepys, were scandalized, as indeed they very well might be. They were more shocked when they found the King took no notice, or no more than passing notice, of the insult. The next morning Charles was observed to be walking with Rochester, and the Earl " as free as ever " in the King's company. Nothing could be done ;

Rochester was a peer of the realm, and it was apt to go hard with gentlemen, even Knights, who sent challenges to peers of the realm. But perhaps Charles might have been more offended if Sir Thomas had not given him so much good advice.

Rochester, however, made some amends. Before April his first banishment had come about; he set out for Paris. Before going he got hold of Henry Killigrew, and "did solemnly ask pardon . . . for the affront he offered his father." Considering that he was a peer, the apology is larger and more handsome than might at first seem. A flicker of that early modesty remained. In Paris it was still further quenched. The English ambassador spoke well of him— "If hereafter he continues to live as discreetly as he has done ever since he was here, he has other good qualities enough to deserve it, and to make himself acceptable wherever he comes." But there had been some trouble. "The King has put the people in prison that injured my Lord Candish and my Lord Rochester, and has expressed a great displeasure against them; and the least that will happen to them, they say, is losing their employments; but all their friends having spoke to me to speak for them to the King, and my Lord Candish desiring it too, I spoke to his most Christian Majesty, and entreated him to forgive them, the English having had all the satisfaction that could be desired."

A larger blaze of laughter tinged with scorn had showed in an earlier episode. There was at the Court another young nobleman, of about the same age but of a different temper, John Sheffield, Earl of Mulgrave, and later, after the death of Villiers, made Duke of Buckinghamshire by Queen Anne. While Henry Wilmot had been pestering Charles for an Earldom in France, John Sheffield's father had sat as a member for Cromwell's council. The Earldom was of Charles I.'s creation; previously the family had been ennobled by Henry VIII. Like Rochester, he was a poet; unlike Rochester, he was not a very good poet. Like Rochester, he was, later, a patron of poets. Dedications were addressed to him from "that stormy pathless world." The phrase, applied to poetry, is Rochester's, not his, and it is suggestive of the difference between them. Rochester might or might not write good verse, but he knew what the world of poetry was. Lord Mulgrave had his rules and conventions, but he hardly knew, for anything that we can see, what passion the rules restrained or what enthusiasms mingled in the convention. Between them both a greater poet than either was insulted and injured. Rochester was perhaps responsible. Even so, in the Paradise of the Poets it is likely that, after some courtesy of pardon, Dryden walks with Rochester rather than Mulgrave.

Late in 1667 or early in 1668, when both of them were still under twenty-one, Lord Mulgrave heard from "some damn'd good-natured friend" or other that Lord Rochester had composed a lampoon upon him. He, like Miss Temple when Miss Hobart hummed in her ear, was moved to an angry, but more haughty, resentment. Rochester, sure of his genius, might have answered a similar insult by another and more bitter epigram. Lord Mulgrave was less certain of his genius and more concerned for his honour. He knew what was due to himself; he took himself solemnly, with a gravity Rochester never achieved. Indeed, all Rochester's indecencies never achieved the supreme spiritual indecency of taking himself in a frigid respect as a person who mattered. If he fought, he fought extravagantly. Lord Mulgrave behaved with decorum, as the age went. He collected a friend, a Colonel Aston, "very mettled," expert in such matters, and sent him to wait on Rochester. The young Earl received him, listened to him, and then, very frankly, set to work to convince the envoy of his own complete innocence. By evidence or protestation he succeeded. Colonel Aston returned to Mulgrave without having delivered the challenge, and assured his chief that Rochester was not to blame. Mulgrave was not to be so easily appeased. For himself he was willing to accept fully the Lord Rochester's denials; merely for his own satisfaction, he was content to ask no more. But his honour also had satisfaction due to it. The lampoon was still current, and it was therefore necessary for Lord Mulgrave to fight someone. It was commonly attributed to Rochester, which was reason and necessity enough for him to fight Rochester. He explained to Colonel Aston, who went back again to the Earl, to explain the solemn demands of Lord Mulgrave's honour—how he fully believed the Earl to be innocent but was fully determined to justify his own reputation before the Court by fighting. Rochester listened, and formally accepted the challenge. Formally, as the challenged party, he laid down the conditions of the duel. He chose to fight on horseback. No objections could be raised by the opposite parties; "it was his part to choose," but "it was a way in England a little unusual," wrote the serious Mulgrave. Rochester named a certain James Porter, acceptable to all three gentlemen, as the second whom he would bring with him. Time and place were fixed ; Colonel Aston withdrew.

Rochester found no intelligence in the affair. He could be thrilled by the dark splendour of presaged death, but he discovered no romantic glory in fighting Lord Mulgrave to heal Lord Mulgrave's wounded self-love. His own egotism was profounder, perhaps, but certainly more careless. He was anxious to justify the universe to himself but not to justify his reputation before the Court. Perversely scornful, he made secret preparations.

Mulgrave and Aston rode out of town to an inn at the little village of Knightsbridge. The offended peer did not wish, if gossip got abroad, to be "secured upon suspicion," and thus be defrauded of his honour-redeeming duel. Still very serious, he half expected also to find the watch on his heels for another reason. He thought that he and Aston must look like disguised highwaymen and that the people of the inn would be alarmed. They were not ; either (as he was driven to suppose) because they were used to highwaymen, or because the two gentlemen looked less like highwaymen than they fancied. The night passed peacefully. In the morning the two rode out to the place of assignation, lightly mounted, to please Lord Rochester's whim. They arrived; they waited; presently they saw two other riders approaching. Incredulously, as these drew nearer, they gazed. It was certainly Rochester, but Rochester in an unexpected display of battle. He came, "extremely well mounted," quite unlike Mulgrave on his light pad, and with him rode not Mr. James Porter but a stranger in the gorgeous uniform of the Life Guards. Lord Mulgrave wanted militancy; Lord Rochester gave him a magnificence of militancy. It looked more like a massacre than a duel.

Colonel Aston hastily protested. The difference in the quality of the mounts was one objection; the unknown quality of the Life Guardsman another. He was "no suitable adversary." The dispute raged. Finally an accommodation was proposed. Colonel Aston accepted the problematic quality of the Guardsman, and Rochester appeared to consent to abandon the superior quality of his mount. He was thought to agree to fight on foot. A move was made towards the next field, where the duel was to take place. But as they all came to the gate, Rochester changed his mind. He said he was ill, and, strictly speaking, unfit to fight at all—certainly unfit to fight on foot. If he fought, it must be on horseback, according to the original terms.

Mulgrave was shocked. He felt Rochester was behaving outrageously. He was un-English. He had insisted on the wrong method of fighting; he had come on the wrong kind of horse; he had brought the wrong kind of second; he was making the wrong kind of remark. He was making nonsense of the whole thing. Everything was ready for the duel and the proper purification of Lord Mulgrave's honour, if only Lord Rochester would get off his horse and fight on foot. True, Rochester had not written the epigram; true, he was not in the least concerned with the affair except in the chatter of the Court. But as the opinion of the Court had provoked Mulgrave in the beginning, so it weighed with him now. He protested that it would make a ridiculous story if they all went home without fighting. Everyone would laugh, and his honour would be more compromised than ever. As the solemn young man urged his plea, his fantastic young opponent looked down on him from his own splendid mount. Mulgrave grew portentous. He urged Rochester to consider carefully, to think better of it "for both our sakes and especially for his own." If, he said, they went home without fighting, he would have to lay the fault on Rochester, by telling the truth of the whole matter. He paused, in solemn expectation of Rochester's solemn recognition of his duty. The Earl on his mount, with his Guardsman second, answered that he submitted to it. "I hope," he added with solemn irony, "that you will not desire the advantage of any man in so weak a condition."

Mulgrave accepted the remark quite seriously. He said that that, of course, tied his hands. The seconds, who had been waiting the result of this (rather improper) discussion between the principals, were waved up, and the matter was explained. The duel was cancelled; separately the parties rode back to London. The honour of Lord Mulgrave, inflamed by the fiasco, was tender, and winced beneath his imagination of laughter and gibes. He heard, or seemed to hear, the mockery of a Court accustomed to duels at this poor semblance of a duel. He and Colonel Aston conferred. Colonel Aston, sitting down while the affair was still vivid in his mind, wrote a full account of every word and circumstance. It was spread abroad. My Lord Mulgrave justified his conduct; my lord Rochester left the account uncontradicted. This, wrote Mulgrave later, " intirely ruin'd his reputation as to Courage

(of which I was really sorry to be the occasion);
tho' nobody had still a greater as to Wit; which
supported him pretty well in the world, notwith-
standing some more accidents of the same kind,
that never fail to succeed one another when once
people know a man's weakness."

"The English," wrote Anthony Hamilton about
that time of another hero, " have in general a sort
of predilection of anything that has the appearance of bravery." But it was not many months
since Rochester, on the testimony of Lord Clifford,
a notable person at Court, had given proofs of
his courage, and fewer since the "much commended" affair of the message in the small boat.
It is likely that while some people thought John
Wilmot was a coward, others—enough to support
Wilmot "pretty well in the world"—thought
that John Sheffield was a fool.

The inflamed quarrel was never eased, nor
the two gentlemen reconciled. Each of them
wrote lines on the other; the dates are unknown,
but it seems likely that Rochester's was the earlier.
It was called " Monster All-Pride," and was a
piece of rhymed invective and not much more.
Even so, it is, on the whole, ruder than Mulgrave's
lines in reply in the *Essay on Satire*, which, composed in 1675, began to be shown publicly in
manuscript in 1679. Each gentleman accused

the other of poor courage, lewd tastes, and bad poetry.

> Tis so lewd a Scribbler, that he writes,
> With as much force to Nature as he fights,

wrote Rochester; and again:

> With equal self conceit too he bears Arms,
> But with that vile success his part performs,
> That he burlesques his trade, and what is best
> In others turns like *Harlequin* in jest.

He ended with an allusion to Mulgrave's red nose:

> Alike at home, abroad, i' th' Camp and Court,
> This Knight o' th' Burning Pestle makes us sport.

Mulgrave attacked in wilder style. He said he despised Rochester (of all things!) for his want of wit; he called him false and cringing (cringing!), "mean in each action, lewd in every limb." As against Rochester's allusion to *The Knight of the Burning Pestle* he brought in a reference to the same author's *A King and No King*.

> For what a Bessus has he always liv'd,
> And his own Kickings notably contriv'd.

He proceeded regretfully:

> I'd like to have left out his poetry,
> Forgot by almost all as well as me.

But he decided to give fourteen lines of abuse to

it : " some Humour, never Wit," " lewdly dull,"
" idle Works," " wretched Texts "—

> 'Mongst forty bad, one tolerable line,
> Without Expression, Fancy, or Design.

Later on, Mulgrave submitted the lines to Alexander Pope, who reduced and concentrated the abuse of the man, omitted the abuse of the poet altogether, and turned the first line of all from " Rochester I despise even for his want of wit " to " Last enter Rochester, of sprightly wit." But then Pope, like Rochester, knew what wit was and what poetry was, and may have had a fair idea of what Mulgrave was. It was, at least, Pope's friend, Swift, who commented on a Character of Mulgrave which in 1733 denounced him as " proud, insolent, covetous, and takes all advantages. In paying his debts unwilling, and is neither esteemed nor beloved." " This character is the truest of any," wrote Swift. It is at least permissible to believe that Rochester also had found, in the fields out towards Knightsbridge, one who was proud and insolent, and took all advantages.

In odd places, at odd times, the quarrel was prolonged ; in that, at any rate, Rochester was consistent. In 1674, three days before Christmas, there was a supper at the Lord Treasurer Danby's.

The King was present, and the drinking was heavy. Henry Savile, one of Rochester's friends, "being very drunck, fel so fowly on Ld: Mulgrave," that Charles at last commanded him to leave the Presence. The next day Mulgrave sent Savile a challenge by the tongue of Lord Middleton. Savile asked Rochester to act for him—it is clear he did not think Rochester had incapacitated himself from acting in affairs of honour.[1] The Earl consented. The affair, however, went no farther. The King for some time, encouraged by his brother, maintained his displeasure, and Savile was forbidden the Court. It is consoling to discover that in the next year the Lord Mulgrave did manage to defend his honour by fighting with a Captain Kirke on a matter connected with Captain Kirke's sister; he was defeated and wounded, and had to keep his chamber for several days.

[1] In 1673 there was nearly a duel between Rochester and Lord Dunbar. Obviously the report of his cowardice—like that of Falstaff, who was an even greater realist than Charles II.—has been much exaggerated.

CHAPTER VI

THE ACTOR AND THE THEATRE

THE history of English drama, especially of the Restoration, has been written often enough. There is room still for a realistic study of it from the patron's point of view. The patron had his day, and it was all he had; succeeding days have belonged to the poets. It was the business of the patron, between his very brief morning and evening, to guess which of the poets who waited on and waited for him would be the reasonable favourite of posterity. Often he did not succeed; posterity has disagreed with and despised him, as in the most famous instance of Dr. Johnson and Lord Chesterfield. The neglect of a year has been repaid by the contempt of the instructed centuries. The centuries, it should be remembered, have been instructed. They have been taught, by docile opinion, what to say. It was not made so easy for the patron. Among half a dozen fellows, carrying manuscripts, avid for recognition, and generally for cash, the patron had to throw one main with Fortune. Fortune, who so often plays with loaded dice, generally saw to it that he lost.

The young wits of the Court—Sedley, Buckhurst, Mulgrave, Rochester—were thronged after this manner. They had obligations to letters which were not fulfilled by their own light interchanges with poetry, and they obligingly fulfilled them. They accepted dedications; they encouraged productions; no doubt they sometimes read manuscript or print, for their interest was not a pose. It was a real interest, even if it were only one of many interests. The pure clarity of their artistic judgment was disturbed by lesser things, by their quarrels or their amours, and even by the enthusiasms of their artistic youth. It was disturbed by quarrels and rivalries among the poets themselves, and the venom of those quarrels was not less sharp than that of the quarrels between the servants of the King in politics or between the servants of God in religion. Sometimes all three conflicts grew together into one, as in the years of the Popish Plot, when the treble anger of Dryden struck politician, priest, and poet, under the names of Achitophel, Corah, and Doeg.

The world was still comparatively quiet when my Lord Rochester was first approached and applauded by the servants of the theatre. His interest at Court was known to be high, and his interest in the theatre real. The fame of his poems and his talk had gone abroad. His epigrams were repeated and his verses copied. By 1670 he was a personage; for the next nine years or so he was a patron. His patronage had two channels: his relation with the poets and his relation with Elizabeth Barry.

It is impossible, however tempting, to identify Elizabeth Barry with Sarah Cooke, even though this means that my lord twice in his life did something like the same thing. In the vagueness of our knowledge it seems safer to assume that he did. He carried away Sarah and her aunt into the country, and there, according to Hamilton, he encouraged her "disposition for the stage." Afterwards, probably by the Earl's care, she entered the King's Company of actors. "She was," said Hamilton, "the prettiest but also the worst actress in the kingdom." On the second occasion of his concern with an actress Rochester reversed the characteristics. He was concerned with the début of Elizabeth Barry, one of the worst-looking but one of the greatest, not only then but, by all accounts, since.

She was said not to be handsome, "her mouth opening most on the right side, which she strove to draw t'other way "; for the rest, she was " middle-sized, and had darkish hair, light eyes, dark eyebrows, and was indifferently plump." Her origin, if we assume she was not Sarah Cooke, is hidden. She asserted that she was the daughter of a barrister named Robert Barry; she was said to have been " waiting-woman to Lady Shelton of Norfolk." If, when she first, at some unknown moment, encountered Rochester, it was not love at first sight, it was at any rate recognition at an early interchange. " By talking with her, he found her Mistress of exquisite charms." Two intellects could play; two energies encountered each other; they needed but a little more greatness on either side to justify the use of the greater words—" two powers." She is supposed to have been about seventeen or eighteen when they met; he was about twenty-five. He loved; he admired. Unlike his other loves, yet not perhaps so unlike what he desired to find in all his loves, she answered his approach with a capacity for action both within and beyond love. They set to work —most happy !—to make something. The young patron and young lover turned to become a young teacher. He began to train his Elizabeth for the stage.

" Madam," he wrote to her once, " you are

stark mad, and therefore the fitter for me to love; and that is the reason, I think, I can never leave to be, Your humble Servant, Rochester." Their combined madness was directed, in that first phase, to the presentation of great imaginations. What he could not find in life, he approximated to on the stage. He himself was no bad actor. Burnet has told us how "he took pleasure to disguise himself, as a *porter*, or as a *beggar*; sometimes to follow some mean amours, which, for the variety of them, he affected. At other times, merely for diversion, he would go about in odd shapes, in which he acted his part so naturally, that even those who were in the secret, and saw him in these shapes, could perceive nothing by which he might be discovered." This capacity he turned to her use. He taught her "to adapt her whole behaviour to the situations of the character." Yes, but he taught her something more, "to seize the passions." "No violence of passion," wrote Colley Cibber of her mature career, "could be too much for her." The thwarted genius of my lord, the immature genius of Elizabeth, came together. "It is thought that, while he lived, he never loved any Person so sincerely as he did Mrs. Barry." "Madam, nothing can ever be so *dear* to me as you are;

and I am so *convinc'd* of this, that I dare undertake to *love* you whilst I *live*. . . ." The thirty-five letters to her that remain reverberate with such sentences. There runs through some of them a suggestion that Rochester was sometimes not quite sure of Elizabeth. . . . " You who love but a *little*, or I who doat to an *Extravagance*; sure, to be half-*kind* is as bad as to be *half*-witted." . . . " I have not *sinn'd* so much as to *deserve* to *live* two whole days without seeing of you." . . . " If your *Anger* continues, show yourself at the *Play*, that I may *look* upon you, and go mad." It would be easy to attribute such phrases to his own extravagance or that of the age. Only Elizabeth Barry was a genius.

It is not, however, to be supposed that Lord Rochester's instructions in dramatic passion, whatever they may have been in actual passion, were by themselves entirely sufficient. He was himself an actor, but not on the stage, and the stage has a technique of its own. In 1674 the two of them risked her appearance at Drury Lane in the King's Company. She was given a small part, and she failed. She could not sing ; her speech and movement were not yet proper to the theatre. At the end of the season her services were declined.

Neither the Earl nor his pupil-mistress allowed

themselves to rest. He made a wager that she would become a good actress. She was subjected to further severe training, and she threw herself into it. In 1675, by his influence with the Bettertons, who then controlled the Duke's Company at Dorset Garden, and were under obligations to Rochester, she was given her second chance, took it, and won. She took the small part of Draxilla in a play called *Alcibiades*, produced on 22nd September before the King, the Queen, and the Duke.

The author of this play was a young man, twenty-three years old, the son of a Sussex rector, who had come up from Oxford to London about four years earlier. His name was Thomas Otway. He had tried to be an actor, and failed; he was now trying to be a dramatist. *Alcibiades*, which was dedicated to the Earl of Middlesex, was not much of a success, but the Duke of York liked it sufficiently to encourage Otway to write another, and the audience liked Mrs. Barry sufficiently to encourage the management to give her another part. Otway liked her more passionately than the crowd. He created for her, at a later period, those forms of Monimia and Belvidera which, in his plays *The Orphan* and *Venice Preserved*, still hover between the front and the back of the English historic stage. Infatuated, he adored and agonized. She gave him nothing, except the use of her genius in the parts which he made for her. She throve by him; he suffered by her. She was Rochester's while Rochester lived, and when Rochester died she became the mistress of Sir George Etherege, the "gentle George" of Rochester's admiration. But for five years the young Otway's passion lies in a dark shadow under the bright dance of the Earl's grandest and most persistent affair. Certainly a woman who was loved for years by Rochester, by Otway, by Etherege, must have been a woman of high capacity.

Possibly Otway did not know of Rochester's and Elizabeth's love. In 1676, the year after *Alcibiades*, he produced, under the encouragement of and with a dedication to the Duke of York, his second play, *Don Carlos*. In the preface, however, he attributed the Duke's interest, and the King's, to Lord Rochester. It was "to him I must in all gratitude confess I owe the greatest part of my good success in this, and on whose Indulgency I extreamly build my hopes of a next." By December in the same year the next, *Titus and Berenice*, an adaptation from Racine, was ready, and was obligingly offered to my lord, who accepted it.

Rochester's patronage of the poets is marked by two things, inconstancy and devastating frankness. His extravagance and his restless intelligence attended him as a patron no less than as a courtier or as a metaphysician. He not only patronized bad poets; he maltreated a good. The first, in the circumstances, could hardly be avoided. Few critics would care to be held to all the enthusiasms of their twenties. The second is no less comprehensible; it is, as we all agree for others, and (if we are wise) for ourselves, no reason why he should not be blamed for it. Properly, unanimously, and continuously, he has been.

His acquaintance with Dryden seems to have begun early. The first evidence we have of their relations is in 1673, when Dryden dedicated a comedy to him, *Marriage à la Mode*. By that time both of them were acknowledged, the poet as a playwright, the nobleman as a patron. It was in the lowly pomp, the modest pride, of his prose that Dryden acknowledged a debt he seemed to feel he owed. It is a tribute to the genius of his prose that, though his dedications are often blamed for servility, yet we hardly feel the fault while reading. Something in the mere style prevents our superiority; our Cascan bluntness is rebuked by his courtesy. True, we would not flatter so; but true also that so we could not flatter. It may be that at any moment the great are more truthful than we, because they have a finer vision. They do perhaps actually see—what lesser men can only pretend to see—a lordliness in noble patrons, a loveliness in royal harlots. They particularize the universal by their mere genius, and it is by no means certain that it is not their gain and their greatness. Mr. Dryden looked at Lord Rochester, and found him good to admire.

In the preface to *Marriage à la Mode*, that admirable comedy of the civilized life of the Restoration, the morality and immorality of which were so different from our fathers' but not so far from ours, Dryden looked at the Earl, and looked back over their friendship. He did not make the details explicit, but he put the main matter clearly enough for us to judge that he felt his honour concerned. He spoke clearly of Rochester having served him almost before any acquaintance and certainly before any entreaty. " I became your Lordship's (if I may venture on the similitude) as the world was made, without knowing him who made it." The Earl's mediations on his behalf, he declared, had been " wholly voluntary." He said he should never forget that Rochester had been careful not only " of my reputation, but of my fortune." On the particular play in question he thanked the Earl for his patronage, his amendments of it for the stage, his commendation of it to the King, who had therefore read it in manuscript. And to the whole noble litany of gratitude he added a gracious colophon : " This nobleness of yours I think myself the rather obliged to own because otherwise it must have been lost to all remembrance : For you are endued with that excellent quality of a frank nature, to forget the good you have done."

The young Rochester was warmed and thrilled by the dedication. He wrote a personal letter to Dryden, and Dryden replied with another, as handsomely phrased as the dedication itself had been. The Earl had gone down to the country ; the letter followed him from town.

" MY LORD,

I have accused my selfe this month together, for not writing to you. I have called my selfe by the names I deserved, of unmannerly and ungratefull. I have been uneasy, and taken up the resolutions of a man, who is betwixt sin and repentance, convinc'd of what he ought to do, and yet unable to do better. At the last, I deferred it so long, that I almost grew hardened in the neglect ; and thought I had suffered so much in your good opinion, that it was in vain to hope I could redeem it. So dangerous a thing it is to be inclin'd to sloath, that I must confess, once for all, I was ready to quit all manner of obligations, and to receive, as if it were my due, the most handsome compliment, couch'd in the best language I have read, and this too from my Lord of Rochester, without shewing myself sensible of the favour. If your Lordship could condescend so far to say all those things to me, which I ought to have say'd to you, it might reasonably be concluded that you had enchanted me to believe these praises, and that I owned them in my silence. 'Twas this consideration that moved me at last to put off my idleness. And now the shame of seeing my selfe overpay'd so much for an ill Dedication, has made me almost repent of my address. I find, it is not for me to contend any way with your Lordship, who can write better than the meanest subject, then I can on the best. I have only engaged my selfe in a new debt, when I had hoped to cancell a part of the old one ; and should either have chosen some other patron, whom it was in my power to have obliged by speaking better of him then he deserv'd, or have made your Lordship only a hearty Dedication of the respect and honour I had for you, without giving you the occasion to conquer me, as you have done, at my own weapon.

"My only relief is, that what I have written is publique, and I am so much of my own friend as to conceal your Lordship's letter; for that which would have given vanity to any other poet, has only given me confusion.

"You see, my Lord, how far you have push'd me; I dare not own the honour you have done me, for fear of shewing it to my own disadvantage. You are that *rerum natura* of your own Lucretius :

Ipsa suis pollens opibus, nihil indiga nostri.

You are above any incense I can give you, and have all the happiness of an idle life, join'd with the good-nature of an active. Your friends in town are ready to envy the leisure you have given your selfe in the country, though they know you are only their steward, and that you treasure up but so much health as you intend to spend on them in winter. In the mean time, you have withdrawn your selfe from attendance, the curse of courts; you may think on what you please, and that as little as you please; for, in my opinion, thinking it selfe is a kind of pain to a witty man; he finds so much more in it to disquiet than to please him."

He went on to Court gossip, inviting Rochester to laugh at the intrigues of the Duke of Buckingham, telling him a story of Sir George Etherege's latest attempt at satire, and with the same familiar courtesy concluded:

"If your Lordship had been in town, and I in the country, I durst not have entertained you with three pages of a letter; but I know they are very ill things which can be tedious to a man, who is fourscore miles from Covent Garden. 'Tis upon this confidence, that I dare almost promise to entertain you with a thousand *bagatelles* every week, and not to be serious in any part of my letter, but that wherein I take leave to call myself your Lordship's

Most obedient servant,

JOHN DRYDEN."

The seriousness was to be of another kind. The very year that had seen the dedication of *Marriage à la Mode* saw the beginning of a separation too much *à la mode*. It has been attributed to two causes, and may well have been due to both.

My lord's extravagance was working widely in him. He had sought vainly for his proper place in the romantic universe, and when he could not find it he was avenging himself on the actual universe both by actions conforming and words reforming. He claimed later that his satires were meant morally; it may be granted that he was divided between enjoyment and disgust. He delighted in the King while he laughed at him; he seduced the royal mistresses while he gibed at them; he indulged his vices while he despised them. With something of the same irritable energy with which he had been militant, and mockingly militant, against Lord Mulgrave, or had half exalted and half scorned Anne Temple, he now turned on his client. Even before *Marriage à la Mode*, Dryden had become famous and popular; on the evidence of the dedication it is to be believed that Rochester had had a hand in making him so. It has even been suggested that it was the Earl's influence which helped to obliterate from the royal memory the poems in honour of Oliver Cromwell, or at least to cancel them by a jest, and that the same influence had assisted Dryden's appointment, in 1670, as laureate and historiographer-royal. It is not impossible; Rochester was no fool in poetry. By 1670 Dryden was famous in heroic tragedy through his *Conquest of Granada*; *Marriage à la Mode* set him up as a master of comedy. Lord Rochester discovered that his own admiration was less pure than he had supposed, or rather he thought he discovered that it was purer. It was one of his biographical contemporaries, who found it less pure and less poetical. According to this testimony, Rochester had urged the poet of his artistic admiration on the world, and the world had docilely and generously applauded. Rochester could not bear the chorus. He would have all approve what he approved, but he would not approve what all approved.

> Scorn all applause the vile Rout can bestow,
> And be content to please those few who know.
> Canst thou be such a vile mistaken thing
> To wish thy *Works* might make a Play-House ring
> With the unthinking Laughter, and poor praise
> Of Fops and Ladies factious for thy Plays?

It seemed that Dryden could. It is possible also that Dryden, for all his generous gratitude, had committed the error of speaking as if God had created him and his genius before Rochester's hand struck in. It is certain, finally, that by some trick of the interchanges between the poets and the lords, in the shifting affairs of that curious borderland between the Court and poetry and bad poetry, where new allegiances and alliances were always being sworn, Mr. Dryden had happened to draw near to the approval of Lord Mulgrave. At twenty-six Rochester was not only incapable of approving what all approved, but still less of approving what Lord Mulgrave approved. His pride forbade him to take second place to his client, and to share his client with Lord Mulgrave. If Dryden and Mulgrave were to admire each other, Rochester, so far as he could, would cast off what admiration he had owned. So far as he could; he could not altogether. " His excellencies " he wrote, in the very poem in which he soon assailed Dryden—

> His Excellencies more than faults abound,
> Nor dare I from his sacred Temples tear
> That Laurel which he best deserves to wear.

But artistic virtue and Court promotion were two separate things. Lord Rochester, keeping the movements of his two hands distinct, wrote with his right, and felt out, rather blindly, for another poet with his left. There were plenty of them; there was a Mr. Elkanah Settle. Mr. Settle had produced one heroic play, *Cambyses, King of Persia*, in 1671. In 1673 he had another ready, *The Empress of Morocco*. The Earl condescended to notice Mr. Settle; it seems even more of a condescension to us than to their contemporaries. Certainly Rochester only had two of Settle's plays to judge by ; we have them all. There was talk of a Court performance of a play. It was current gossip that Rochester had persuaded Charles to approve the *Empress.* The slight to Dryden, laureate and playwright, was marked. It is the more curious that, at the first performance, a prologue was provided by Lord Mulgrave. Perhaps Lord Rochester had lost interest in the details of the production ; perhaps the King had, carelessly but clearly, commanded him to be civil. The two gentlemen, after all, had to move always in the same circle. For the second performance, however, Rochester himself supplied the prologue, a pleasing trifle, spoken by the Lady Elizabeth Howard. It has the peculiar merit of touching more lightly on the King's multitudinous loves than was my lord's habit. The Lady Elizabeth, turning from the listening courtiers to His Majesty, exclaimed, sinking in courtesies :

> "But why do I descend to lose a Prayer,
> On those small Saints in Wit ? The God sits there."

It was a Greek, Roman, or Restoration-Roman God. Charles was admonished that only old age would set him free from the "soft captivity" of women ; he was reminded (great Prince) that "'gainst us still you have made a weak defence."

But then the Lady Elizabeth, melting under the royal eyes, was then taught to say that

> "Love is our Commander and your Friend.
> Our Victory your Empire more assures,
> For Love will ever make the Triumph Yours."

On another occasion the Earl, in a set of verses called *The Royal Angler*, put the same thing in different language :

> Howe'er weak and slender be the string,
> Bait it with *Whore*, and it will hold a King.

Neither statement was, finally, true of Charles Stuart. But he sat in the royal chair, and listened with his usual good temper to the Lady Elizabeth's pleasant and amorous humility. The play was applauded ; Settle was established. Alas, *c'est le second, le troisième, jusqu'au l'infini pas qui coûte.* For a year Settle's reputation divided honours with Dryden. My lord had forced him on the Court, the town, and the University of Cambridge. In the last two places " the younger fry inclined to Elkanah," said the sardonic critic John Dennis. Dryden was sufficiently moved, by Settle or by Rochester's support of Settle, to ally himself with two other minor dramatists, John Crowne and Thomas Shadwell, in a pamphlet attack on him. The dispute lingered on until, seven years after,

Dryden dealt the *coup de grâce* in the lines on Doeg in *Absalom and Achitophel*.

But long before Dryden destroyed Settle immortally, Rochester had abandoned him mortally. The *Empress* was a grand success, at Court, at the public theatre to which it was transferred, and as a publication. The happy author had his hour of glory. Visions and dreams ran beckoning before him. The Lord Rochester had taken him up. Alas! when, two years later, he had his next play ready—it was *Love and Revenge*—my lord had dropped him down. He needed for his own honour, if not for himself alone, a good poet. The world and Lord Mulgrave approved of Dryden, and Rochester would not. But the world also approved of Settle, and Rochester neither would nor could. He was angry with the world.

Settle was left to settle in the mud of controversy and the City. He ended, poor man! after a taste of success, after writing for and against the Popish Plot, at a booth in Bartholomew Fair, and died later in Charterhouse—long after, in 1724, when George I. sat, under the direction of the great Families, on the English throne, and Johnson was a lad of fifteen at Lichfield. George I. and Johnson were both remote, when in 1675 the young Princess Mary, daughter of the Duke of

York, and a girl of thirteen, desired the pleasure of a Masque. It was the business of the Laureate to provide Masques for the Court, but Rochester once more intervened. Among his pocket poets was a nice little creature called John Crowne, who, in 1672, had dedicated to the Earl an heroic play, *Charles the Eighth*. It is quite impossible not to feel Crowne was a nice little fellow, his preluding remarks to his plays are so happily frank. They do not bear the false humility of Settle nor the stately subordination of Dryden. He admitted that he "had not the honour of much acquaintance with your Lordship," but he knew some of the Earl's poems ("I have seen in some little sketches of your pen excellent Masteries") and he had heard his epigrams repeated ("I have been entertained by others with the wit which your Lordship, with a gentle and careless freedom, sprinkles in your ordinary converse"). As for the play of *Charles the Eighth*, he said, frankly and justly, that it was "a play in verse (and an ill one too)," and admitted he was surprised it had so few enemies. It may have been this agreeable candour that captivated my lord, as a change from more conventional obeisances.

At any rate, the requests of the Princess, the Duke, and the Earl were conveyed to Crowne.

The history of the Masque, according to his own account, is not unamusing. The great personages required it in a hurry. " In they burst, those people of importance." It must be written at once, and be ready in four weeks or less. It was to be presented for seven ladies, " and of those seven only two were to appear in men's habits." It was to have Choruses—Shepherds, Gypsies, Satyrs, " Bacchusses," and Africans. The prospect of inventing a suitable entry for Africans rather perplexed Crowne, but he did his best. It was to have songs, and dances, and a dramatic prologue. It was to be joyous but refined—for the Princess Mary and the Princess Anne were to take part. And they all wanted to know, in " some few hours," what it was going to be about. In a great hurry the neat little Crowne ransacked his brain and his shelves, and decided on the Rape of Calisto by Jupiter, because Calisto could stand for Chastity, and the Princess Mary could act Chastity, and so far the way was clear. He flung himself into the work ; he did his best with the difficulties and dangers of the assault on a Chastity who was also a Princess. He wrote it, finished it, and submitted it. The royal and lordly producers found some of it too coarse, and he pulled bits of it to pieces and did them again. After all this rush, it was found that the production itself required more time than had been supposed. "Those on whom the dancing and music depended, found it required time to do anything in perfection ; but I, not knowing it would be so deferred, finished my part within the time first allotted me." " By these means," Mr. Crowne added simply, " I was forced upon a brisk dullness, quick but flat." [1]

Between the second and third performances—it was given on a number of occasions—he rewrote it, and it was relearnt, to satisfy himself and encourage his audience, who had most of them drifted in and out of the rehearsals. Even so, it was not very good. "It is enough to tell you," wrote Mr. Crowne, " that it was written by me ; and it would be very strange if a bad writer should write well." He turned, with a gracious humility, towards Dryden : "Had it been written by him, to whom, by the double right of place and merit, the honour of the employment belonged, the pleasure had been in all kinds complete."

The difficulties, in fact, are still here and there obvious. In the Prologue, for example, in a dialogue between the River Thames and the

---

[1] Some playwright, defending his own play, said it was written in only three weeks. "How the devil," said Lord Rochester, " could he be so long about it ? "

Genius of England, Thames laments that Augusta, by which London was signified, is weeping, after which follows this stage direction :

> "The following stanza is properly part of the Genius's speech, being a pertinent reply to Thames ; but being set extreme pleasantly, and for a treble voice, it was sung by Thames."

Thames had to be made feminine, and Europe masculine, also owing to the exigencies of the cast. Thames was impersonated by Mrs. Davis, one of the King's mistresses, and Europe by Mr. Hart, the acknowledged lover of Lady Castlemaine ("by this means," wrote Pepys, "she is even with the King's love to Mrs. Davis"). Thames was attended by Peace and Plenty, Peace being taken by Mrs. Knight, who was another of Charles's mistresses, and Plenty by Mrs. Butler, who, astonishingly, was not. It is pleasant to think where, and by whom, that great maxim of honest Liberalism had its first rise.

Of the other performers, the Princess Mary being reserved for Calisto or Chastity, the Princess Anne had created for her the part of Nyphe, a chaste friend of Chastity. On the other hand, Juno was presented by Anne, Countess of Sussex, acknowledged as the King's illegitimate daughter; and a minuet was danced by the Duke of Monmouth, the King's illegitimate son. Two Maids of Honour took speaking parts: Sarah Jennings, as Mercury, and Margaret Blagge, as Diana. The taste of Miss Blagge provides a final ludicrous, pathetic, and noble interlude in the whole affair. She was a serious young lady, attendant on the Queen, and she did not enjoy her part. She was envied and mocked. " Now you know I am to turne the other cheeke," she wrote to the staid John Evelyn,[1] " nor take I notice of it." During the performances, Evelyn recounts that " when she was not on the stage, she was in the Tireing-roome, where severall Ladyes her companions were railing with the gallants trifleingly enough till they were called to re-enter, she, under pretence of conning her next part, was retired into a corner, reading a booke of Devotion without at all concerning herselfe or mingling with the young company—as if she had no further part to act who was the principal person of the comedy." . . . " For the rest of that dayes triumph I have a particular account still

[1] He had dined with Rochester in 1670 at Windsor, among other lords, and observed his " profane wit."

by me of the rich apparel she had on her, amounting besides the Pearles and Pretious Stones, to above three hundred pounds, but of all which she immediately disposed her selfe soe soone as ever she could get clear of the Stage. Without complimenting any creature or trifling with the rest who staid the collation and refreshment that was prepar'd, away she slips like a spiritt to Berkley House, and to her little oratorye; whither I waited on her, and left her on her knees thanking God that she was delivered from this vanity, and with her Saviour againe, never, says she, will I come within this temptation more whilst I breath."

Calisto was in 1675; after its performance Rochester lost interest in Crowne. It was rumoured, not improbably, that he abandoned him for the same reason that he abandoned Dryden, because the poor little fellow became popular. A similar story was told of Dryden himself. "He would compliment Crowne when a play of his failed, but was very cold to him if he met with success. He sometimes used to say that Crowne had some genius, but then he added always, that his father and Crowne's mother were very well acquainted."

There had been other dedications. Nathaniel Lee had offered *Nero, Emperor of Rome*, and a writer who was of another social level, Sir Francis Fane, had crowned his comedy, *Love in the Dark*, with Rochester's " crested and prevailing name." It was crested there with a unique tribute. Sir Francis was the first to grow morally better in the Earl's company. He declared, rather surprisingly, that he always returned from it " a better Christian." It is to be feared that Sir Francis meant by " Christian " nothing more at best than socially moral; even that is surprising enough. But it cannot wholly be neglected; it is not the phrase of a needy petitioner. In the wildest period of the Earl's life there was, it seems, something which for a moment touched one obscure mind to a loftier sense of its duties and decencies.

Meanwhile the Earl amused himself at intervals with saying in verse what he thought of his clients. He was much more civil to his Court friends than to mere authors. Buckhurst, Sedley, Etherege, were all praised; Sedley, notably, for having

> that prevailing gentle art
> That can with a resistless Charm impart
> The loosest Wishes to the chastest Heart.

Sedley, indeed, might have been pleased with the compliment. But it was not alone the compliment that concerned its maker, it was the opposition and the combination. Through Rochester's poetry there runs that metaphysical sense of the combination of opposites. One of his more famous poems, *Upon Nothing*, contains it:

> Something the gen'ral Attribute of all,
> Sever'd from thee, its sole Original,
> Into thy boundless self must undistinguish'd fall.
>
> Yet something did thy mighty power command,
> And from thy fruitful Emptiness's hand,
> Snatch'd Men, Beasts, Birds, Fire, Air, and Land.
>
> Matter, the wicked'st offspring of thy Race,
> By Form assisted, flew from thy embrace,
> And Rebel Light obscur'd thy reverend dusky face.

The still more famous *All my past Life* has it in an even more poignant sense:

> All my past Life is mine no more,
>   The flying Hours are gone:
> Like transitory Dreams giv'n o'er,
> Whose Images are kept in store,
>   By Memory alone.
>
> The Time that is to come is not;
>   How can it then be mine?
> The present Moment's all my Lot;
> And that, as fast as it is got,
>   *Phillis*, is only thine.
>
> Then talk not of Inconstancy,
>   False Hearts, and broken Vows;
> If I, by Miracle, can be
> This live-long Minute true to thee,
>   'Tis all that Heav'n allows.

The thrill of that poem is a thrill of fidelity, and not of infidelity, but the fidelity is that of the whole concentrated instant. "The flying moment" has achieved, "by miracle," the completeness of all, and though whatever good may be gained by a temporal perseverance may be lost to this spirit, yet no temporal change can invalidate the supreme victory of that spirit in its moment. It was to such a concentration that in his lordliest moments Lord Rochester's desires were directed, and it can hardly be doubted that it was because they aimed at rhetoric rather than pure passion that he despised his poets. He made mistakes himself in poetry, but he demanded and sought the greatest.

> Oh but the World will take offence thereby!
> Why, then the World shall suffer for't and not I.
> Did e'er this saucy World and I agree
> To let it have its beastly Will on me?

He was rude and yet respectful to Dryden. He was rude without being at all respectful to Settle, Crowne, Otway, and Lee, to say nothing of Shadwell: "Crowne's tedious sense," "blund'ring Settle," "puzzling Otway," were compared disadvantageously with Dryden, or denounced in other lines by themselves.

There was one other poet, though not a

dramatist, who should be mentioned, a poet whom Rochester and Dryden separately praised. In the Whitgift School at Croydon was an usher named John Oldham, who wrote verse. By some accident, so the story goes, verse of his writing came, in the year 1675 or thereabouts, to the eyes of Rochester, Buckhurst, and Sedley. They read and applauded; with an enthusiasm readers might aspire to approximate, they determined to seek him out. One day a whole group of noble gentlemen magnificently and unexpectedly descended on Croydon and the school. A servant, sent with Lord Rochester's compliments to Mr. Oldham, and a request that he would show himself, by mistake delivered it to the Headmaster. The cause of the visit was not particularized. Oldham would know that only one thing could have brought so distinguished a company. The Headmaster, who knew nothing of his usher's capacities, hastily made himself as presentable as possible, and tottered in. He made his bows and began to make a speech, decently grateful for the honour done him, and obviously entirely ignorant of the reason. The fine gentlemen, catching the absurdity, began to laugh, until "Lord Dorset, observing the confusion of the man and the laughing gravity of Lord Rochester," explained. The old gentleman escaped; the usher was sent for; another admirer was added to Rochester's train, and the future obscenities of Mr. Oldham's verse were laid to Rochester's charge, for he " it was thought had wit and wickedness to debauch the most pious hermit." Oldham at least imitated one of my lord's impromptus at the beginning of one of his satires (" By hell, 'twas bravely done " is too like " By heaven, 'twas bravely done "), and wrote a pastoral elegy on him under the name of Bion. Three years later Oldham himself died, and was more greatly honoured by one of the magnificent openings of Dryden—" Farewell, too little and too lately known."

The recurrence of that name introduces the episode which was to be the last in Rochester's life of literary patronage and despite.

In 1679 occurred the attack on Dryden. Rochester's own attitude towards Dryden and Dryden's patron Mulgrave had remained consistent. He despised Mulgrave—he probably despised him too much to hate him. He despised Dryden, probably as a client and friend of Mulgrave's, but he did not despise Dryden's poetry. A desultory, critical war had spread between them. One of Rochester's poems had been called "An Allusion to Horace: the Tenth Satire of the First Book"; it was that which began

> Well, Sir, 'tis granted, I said D——'s rhymes
> Were stol'n, unequal, nay dull, many times.

In 1678 Dryden's *All for Love* was presented and published. It was dedicated to the Earl of Danby, then Treasurer, and the preface contained something very like a retaliatory attack on Rochester. No names were mentioned, but after an exposition of his play Dryden turned off, by way of the French drama, into a general attack on the wits who desired to be thought poets and judges of poetry:

"From hence it comes that so many satires on poets, and censures of their writings, fly abroad. Men of pleasant conversation (at least esteemed so), and endued with a trifling kind of fancy, perhaps helped out with some smattering of Latin, are ambitious to distinguish themselves from the herd of gentlemen, by their poetry—— . . . And is not this a wretched affectation, not to be contented with what fortune has done for them, and sit down quietly with their estates, but they must call their wits in question, and needlessly expose their nakedness to public view? Not considering that they are not to expect the same approbation from sober men, which they have found from their flatterers after the third bottle. If a little glittering in discourse has passed them on us for witty men, where was the necessity of undeceiving the world ? . . . We who write, if we want the talent, yet have the excuse that we do it for a poor subsistence ; but what can be urged in their defence, who, not having the vocation of poverty to scribble, out of mere wantonness take pains to make themselves ridiculous ? . . . while they are so eager to destroy the fame of others, their ambition is manifest in their concernment ; some poem of their own is to be produced, and the slaves are to be laid flat with their faces on the ground, that the monarch may appear in the greater majesty. . . . Mæcenas took another course, and we know he was more than a great man, for he was witty too : But finding himself far gone in poetry, which Seneca assures us was not his talent, he thought it his best way to be well with Virgil and with Horace ; that at least he might be a poet at the second hand ; and we see how happily it has succeeded with him ; for his own bad poetry is forgotten, and their panegyrics of him still remain. But they who should be our patrons are for no such expensive ways to fame ; they have much of the poetry of Mæcenas, but little of his liberality. . . . Some of their little zanies yet go further; for they are persecutors even of Horace himself, as far as they are able, by their ignorant and vile imitations of him; by making an unjust use of his authority, and turning his artillery against his friends. But how would he disdain to be copied by such hands! I dare answer for him, he would be more uneasy in their company, than he was with Crispinus, their forefather, in the Holy Way."

He quoted, in the original Latin, from the very Satire to which Rochester had "alluded." "With what scorn," Dryden wrote on, "would [Horace] look down on such miserable translators, who make doggerel of his Latin, mistake his meaning, misapply his censures, and often contradict their own? . . . For my part, I would wish no other revenge, either for myself, or the rest of the poets, from this rhyming judge of the twelvepenny gallery, this legitimate son of Sternhold, than that he would subscribe his name to his censure, or (not to tax him beyond his learning) set his mark: For, should he own himself publicly, and come from behind the lion's skin, they whom he condemns would be thankful to him, they whom he praises would choose to be condemned; and the magistrates, whom he has elected, would modestly withdraw from their employment, to avoid the scandal of his nomination. The sharpness of his satire, next to himself, falls most heavily on his friends, and they ought never to forgive him for commending them perpetually the wrong way, and sometimes by contraries. If he have a friend, whose hastiness in writing is his greatest fault, Horace would have taught him to have minced the matter, and to have called it readiness of thought, and a flowing fancy ; . . . But he would never have allowed him to have called a slow man hasty, or a hasty writer a slow drudge. . . ."

"Hasty Shadwell and slow Wycherley," Rochester had written. Thus closing in on the Earl, Dryden at last picked him up and threw him away. "I leave him to interpret this by the benefit of his French version on the other side, and without further considering him, than I have the rest of my illiterate censors, whom I have disdained to answer, because they were not qualified for judges."

In that small world of poets and courtiers, where Dryden was the King's laureate and Rochester the gentlemen's, there were minds enough to relish all such attacks and tongues enough to publish them. A letter from Rochester in the country—probably of 1679—

to Savile in town remains,[1] in which the Earl wrote :

"You write me word, That I'm out of favour with a certain Poet, whom I have ever admir'd, for the disproportion of him and his Attributes : He is a Rarity which I cannot but be fond of, as one would be of a Hog that could fiddle, or a singing Owl. If he falls upon me at the Blunt, which is his very good Weapon in Wit, I will forgive him, if you please, and leave the Repartee to *Black Will*, with a Cudgel. And now, Dear *Harry*, if it may agree with your Affairs, to shew yourself in the Country this Summer, contrive such a Crew together, as may not be asham'd of passing by *Woodstock*."

At the end of that year, 1679, Savile was in Paris and Rochester back in London. The satire upon which Lord Mulgrave had been engaged, and which he is supposed to have submitted to Dryden for improvement, appeared. Rochester wrote to his friend :

[1] This "Black Will" letter has generally been assumed to have been provoked by the Mulgrave satire. But this has the slight difficulty that it was certainly the satire which Rochester sent to Savile ; in which case it can hardly have been that to which he was referring in the "Black Will" reply. The energy of Dryden's attack in the *All for Love* preface has been, perhaps, a little underrated. The tentative order suggested in the text would smooth the progress of the affair.

"I have sent you herewith a Libel, in which my own share is not the least; the King having perus'd it, is no ways disatisfy'd with his: the Author is apparently Mr. (Dryden), his Patron my Lord (Mulgrave) having a Panegerick in the midst, upon which happen'd a handsome Quarrel between his L—— and *Mr. B*—— at the Dutchess of *P*——; she call'd him: The Heroe of the Libel, and Complimented him upon having made more Cuckolds, than any man alive; to which he answer'd, She very well knew one he never made, nor never car'd to be imploy'd in making.— Rogue and Bitch ensued, till the King, taking his Grand-father's Character upon him, became the Peace-maker. I will not trouble you any longer, but beg you still to Love

Your Faithful,
Humble Servant,
ROCHESTER."

Rochester was still very much a peer of England; if he were courteous to his inferiors it was by his grace and not of their deserving. It was said that he chid his servants so agreeably that it was a pleasure to hear him. His servants, however, would be wise not to assume any fundamental equality; the Lord Rochester's abstract notions of man could hardly have endured that,

If a commoner, even a commoner whose verses Lord Rochester admired, insulted a peer, the peer, if he deigned to take any notice, sent footmen to correct him. To distinguish him even so much was almost a compliment, it was doing the fellow too much honour to enable him to boast that he had moved some great gentleman to avenge himself vicariously.

We do not certainly know what happened. Rochester had written easily from Woodstock to Savile of what he would do. On Monday, 18th December 1679, Dryden, walking home from his evening levee at Will's Coffee-House, through Rose Street, Covent Garden, was attacked and beaten by three bullies. The affair made a good deal of noise—"an unkind trespass by which not only he but the commonwealth of learning may receive an injury," said a London newspaper. The Duke of Buckingham, the Duchess of Portsmouth, and Rochester were all suspected. Fifty pounds reward was offered to anyone who would discover the offenders, and a free pardon if he had been a principal or accessory. "The cudgell'd poet" became the phrase of Dryden's enemies; "a Rose-alley ambuscade" of his friends. That Rochester knew of the intention is more than probable; that he was its instigator is not certain, but not improbable. His guilt in that matters the less when it is remembered that he certainly mocked Dryden afterwards—" who'd be a Wit in Dryden's cudgelled Skin?" It is perhaps a little more in accord with his general character and with the character of his satire that he should laugh at something of which he had not been the direct cause. The most admirable part of the whole episode came long after. In 1693 Dryden, in the dedication of his own *Essay on Satire* to Buckhurst, wrote: "The subject of this book confines me to Satire; and in that, an author of your own quality (whose ashes I will not disturb) has given you all the commendation which his self-sufficiency could afford to any man: *The best good man, with the worst-natur'd Muse.* In that character, methinks, I am reading Johnson's verses to the memory of Shakespeare; an insolent, sparing, and invidious panegyric: where good nature, the most god-like commendation of a man, is only attributed to your person, and denied to your writings."

"Whose ashes I will not disturb."

CHAPTER VII

INTERLUDES IN THE COUNTRY

BY reason of his love for his wife, or of his variable health, or of the King's anger with his poems, or of his wish for leisure to write more poems, or merely to take part in a scene played in front of another backcloth, the Earl of Rochester spent a good deal of his time in the country. The Countess of Rochester spent all her time there. It was, in those days, a not uncommon arrangement. He had been appointed Keeper of the King's Game in Oxfordshire in 1668; in 1674 he was made Ranger of Woodstock Park, and afterwards Keeper. There was some difficulty between him and his relations, the Lees, but Rochester was successful. The Ranger's Lodge became his usual home in the country. For the country as the country the Earl seems to have cared little enough. The primrose hardly caught his eye even as a primrose, much less as anything more; and counter-marching clouds left his Restoration mind unaffected.

He could, of course, turn a verse about glades or what not. He could write poems about

Chloris under a willow, or even as a keeper of pigs. He could carry the invocation of Celia's tender mercies, the rebuke of her ingratitude, and the final mingled threat and entreaty, among the boughs and the books, and imply his own resemblance to the stream and hers to the flowers upon the banks, which, if it becomes stormy, will be destroyed. In one poem, on a Pastoral Courtship, he reviewed the small fauna of the woods, and the lover reassured his mistress concerning serpents, toads, spiders, frogs, snails, and other terrors:

> No Wasp nor Hornet haunts this Grove,
> Nor Pismire to make Pimples rise
> Upon thy smooth and ivory thighs.

"Ivory" was perhaps a little casual in relation to the idea of stings. But Lord Rochester—who was as modern as Mr. Joyce in his investigations or as Mr. Aldous Huxley in his desire to reconcile the intellectual and the sensational—was sometimes modern in his verse, and preferred the emotional to the logical connexion. In fact, cedars and junipers suggested women to Lord Rochester as naturally and inevitably as the fallen yew suggested religion to Francis Thompson, or the storm-swept oak the grand scope of the human heart to Wordsworth. He carried down to Adderbury or to Woodstock the same preoccupations which possessed him in town. It was men and women—and still more men and women in their relation to Lord Rochester—with whom only he was concerned; they, and the imaginative life where he still desired unity; they, and pre-eminently, in the country, Lady Rochester.

He wrote to her from town; had we her side of the correspondence, the movement of their relations would be more easily observed. His own letters vary continually; their most marked characteristic is their brevity, and their second the many reasons which he gives for not writing at more length or for not coming to her. He is in bed; he has been in waiting on the King; he has something to tell her, but at present it is not fit to mention it; he is dull and will not be tedious to her; he must be at Court; he must not be "too wise about my own follies." In his letters, indeed, except occasionally, Rochester was not quite at his best. He had no scope. There is an impatience with the method; perhaps, except spasmodically, there was a dislike of self-committal. It may be that precisely that attention to words and that sense of them which made him a good poet made him a bad correspondent. He was no more prepared to abandon himself on paper than in life to anything he had so far known, unless indeed it were to that strong genius, Mrs. Barry. On the other hand, there is in the letters to his wife, at their best, an easy and happy humour ; and at their worst an offended humour. His chief affections perhaps had hardly determined their own course. He was not yet thirty, and at that age sensation is hardly certain of its true monogamy. Besides, he was partly responsible not merely for Lady Rochester's happiness but for her comfort. It was not only a question of money. He sent her what he could ; he was never a miser. But there was his mother. It is impossible not to believe that he perversely refused to be actively intelligent about his wife's relations with the Dowager.

" Wonder not that I have not writt to you all this while for it was hard for mee to know what to write, upon severall accounts, but in this I will only desire you not to bee to much amazd at the thoughts my mother has of you, since being meer immaginations they will as easily vanish as they were groundlessly created, for my owne part I will make it my endeavour they may, what you desired of mee in your other letter shall punctually bee perform'd ; you must I think obey my mother in her commands to waite on her at Alesbury as I tould you in my last letter. I am very dull at this time & therefore thinke it pitty in this humour to testify my selfe to you any farther only deare wife,

    I am your humble servant,
        ROCHESTER."

It seems unlikely that Lord Rochester could seriously have believed that the mere fact of such imaginations being groundless would cause them to vanish. Nor, of course, did he. But it served; it sounded philosophical, and almost Hobbist. If imaginations—even the Dowager's about her daughter-in-law—were indeed only the decaying sense, they ought surely to vanish. Alas, the Dowager did not rule herself by Mr. Hobbes; she was religious; besides, the decaying sense renewed itself by too frequent visits. On one occasion the Earl escaped from the two ladies, excusing himself in a letter:

" TO MY WIFE,
Runn away like a rascall without taking leave, deare wife, it is an unpollisht way of proceeding wch a modest man ought to bee asham'd of. I have left you a prey to your owne immagina-

tions amongst my relations, the worst of damnations; but there will come an houer of deliverance, till when, may my mother bee mercifull unto you, soe I committ you to what shall ensue, woman to woman, wife to mother, in hopes of a future appearance in glory; the small share I can spare you out of my packett I have sent as a debt to Mrs. Rouse, within a weeke or ten dayes I will returne you more, pray write as often as you have leisure to

Y^r

ROCHESTER.

Remember me to Nan, and my Ld Willmott.

You must present my service to my cosins. I intend to bee att the deflowring of my neice Ellen if I heare of it. Excuse my ill paper and my ill manners to my mother they are both the best the place and age will afford———"

In view of this, almost the cruellest thing that Rochester ever did was to conjoin them in his will, and leave the responsibility to the Countess. "For the better assurance of a happy correspondence between my deare mother and my deare wife, I doe appoint to my mother and wife the gardianship of my sonn till he attaine the age of one and twentie, so long as my wife shall remaine unmarried and friendly live with my mother; always provided that if my wife shall marrie or wilfully seperate herselfe from my mother, that then this her gardianship shall determine."

Lady Rochester herself had a capable pen:

"If I could have been troubled att any thing when I had the happyness of resceiving a letter from you I should be soe because you did not name a time when I might hope to see you: The uncertainty of which very much aflicts me whether this ode kind of proceeding be to try my patience or obedyence I cannot guesse, but I will never faile of ether where my duty to you requier them, I doe not think you design staying att Bath now that it is like to be soe full and God knows when you will find in your heart to leave the place you are in: pray consider with your selfe wheather this be a reasonable way of proceeding and be pleased to lett me know what I am to expect for thear being soe short a time betwixt this and the sitting of the Parlemant I am confident you will find soe much bussiness as will not allow you to come into the country thearfore pray lay your commands upon me what I am to doe and though it be to forgett my children and the long hopes I have lived in of seeing you, yet I will endeavour to obey you or in the memory only torment my selfe without giving you the trouble of puting you in mind that thear lives such a creature as your faithfull humble . . ."

But at the game of pretending that death would solve all problems her husband could easily outplay her.

" My most neglected Wife, till you are a much respected Widdow, I find you will scarce be a contented Woman, and to say noe more than the plaine truth I doe endeavour soe fairly to doe you that last good service that none but the most impatient would refuse to rest satisfied. What evill Angell Enimy to my repose does inspire my Lady Warr to visitt you once a yeare & leave you bewitch'd for elev'n months after ? I thanke my God that I have the Torment of the Stone upon mee (wch are noe small ones) rather than that unspeakable one of being an eye witness to y^r uneasinesses ; Doe but propose to mee any reasonable thing upon Earth I can do to sett you att quiett but it is like a madd woman to lye roaring out of paine and never confess in what part it is : these three yeares have I heard you continually complain, nor has itt ever bin in my pow'r to obtain the knowledge of any considerable cause ; confident I shall nott have the like affliction three yeares hence, but that repose. I owe to a surer freind than you; when the time comes you will grow Wiser, though I feare nott much happyer."

It seems that the two young creatures, in fact, like others, quarrelled and made it up and complained and forgave and were at odds and at one, and vibrated happily and unhappily in answer to each other. They had four children—Anne in 1669; Charles in 1670; Elizabeth in 1674; Mallet (a girl) in 1674 or 1675. "May we not believe" that the name given to the last indicates a happy recollection of the days before marriage? We certainly may, if we choose; there is nothing to show.

Lady Rochester had her diversions.[1] She too wrote poetry, and she too had an interest in man's nature and destiny.

Her search for its meaning was more orthodox than her husband's. While he argued against dogma in London, she complicated hers in the country. Soon after their marriage, when they

---

[1] Among them, according to Aubrey, was toxicology. He says that the second wife of Sir John Denham, author of *Cooper's Hill*, who once in a distemper " went to the King and told him he was the Holy Ghost," " was poisoned by the hands of Co. of Roc. with chocolate." The Dowager Countess, if this were so, was unusually fortunate.

were both at Adderbury, Rochester found himself in need of money, and desired to mortgage temporarily part of the estate. He heard that there was that day at the parsonage, come upon business with him, the same Stephen College who, not long before, had served in his troop at Chatham. College was sent for and asked if he could carry a letter, " if you are at leisure this afternoon." " My lord, I am at leisure to serve you." Off, therefore, went College with the letter. It was to a certain Thomson, who lived in a Roman Catholic family, the Brooks. Thomson was reported to be a priest, though College, who had lived in the house for six months, had never seen him " at Popish service or worship." If, however, there is anything madder than human action it is human credulity; in this extraordinary universe the two seem continually to be striving each to outdo the other. Thomson was supposed to be a priest. There, according to College's own showing, at his execution years afterwards, his connexion with the affair ceased. It is not impossible, however, that that letter was the beginning of conversion. Either Thomson or the Brooks, becoming involved in Lord Rochester's finance, may have also been involved in Lady Rochester's faith. By 1677 it was known that she was a Papist. A Somersetshire man (there were estates of Rochester's in Somerset) was in that year lodging in London with a Mr. Peters at the Crown and Anchor in Wych Street, off the Strand. College lived at the back of the house, and "dropped in" on Mr. Peters one Sunday evening. He "entered into discourse" concerning Lord Rochester and his lady, extolling the latter and vilifying the former. "I told him I heard my lady was turned Papist. He asked me what I meant by a Papist." The conversation then became theological.

College never quite got free of the suspicion, in spite of his activities on the other side during the days of the Popish Plot, when his enthusiasm earned him the title of "the Protestant Joiner." He distributed ribbons; he sold flails; he made a Protestant song—the Raree Show—and set it to the tune of one of Lord Rochester's songs. He made himself prominent, and suffered the result, since when the King was able to enjoy something of his own once more, College was arrested for seditious language, tried at Oxford, and executed. The conversion of Lady Rochester was not made a part of the indictment, but it was very much in the air again, since she had died of a stroke of apoplexy some days earlier. The rumours may have originally encouraged College to be so ostentatiously Protestant;

their revival encouraged the Attorney-General to comment at the trial on that ostentation:
"I believe if this gentleman were examined thoroughly, he would be found to be one of the same stamp [as a certain Papist], and acted by the same principle."

A Papist, at any rate, Lady Rochester became; it must have added to the difficulties with the Dowager. But not, it seems, with her husband, whose satirical comments on the Roman Church in his poems did not extend to his letters. There was, as we know later from the Dowager, a "popish physician" in the Ranger's Lodge; it seems likely that Lady Rochester brought him there. The Earl, in London, argued differently. Later he told his chaplain, or the chaplain said that he did:

"I have had some checks and warnings considerable from within, but still struggled with 'em, and so wore them off again. The most observable that I remember was this: One day at an Atheistical Meeting, at a person of Qualities, I undertook to manage the Cause, and was the principal Disputant against God and Piety, and for my performances received the applause of the whole company; upon which my mind was terrible struck, and I immediately reply'd thus to my self. Good God! that a Man, that walks upright, that sees the wonderful works of God, and has the uses of his senses and reason, should use them to the defying of his Creator!"

The reply is certainly the chaplain's and not Rochester's. But "the applause of the whole company" put him out of humour with Atheism as a similar cause had disgusted him with Dryden. When everyone was impious it was time for the Earl of Rochester to be "terrible struck" with the justice of piety. Fruition itself in those circumstances disappointed him.

For reasons of health, if not of love, sometimes my lord came down to the country. In 1671 his eyes were already troubling him. A correspondent wrote from town, "I am very sorry you find your eyes can neither endure wine nor water"; six years afterwards, he himself wrote to Savile, "I am almost blind." It need not be taken too literally, but it was the kind of thing to irritate and thwart his temper—another sort of disappointed fruition. But how to find real fruition? In the country he amused himself as best he could; *mutatis mutandis*, in the same manner as in town, though more civilly. "He was wont to say," said Aubrey, "that when he came to Brentford the devill entered into him and never left him till he came to the country again to Adderbury or Woodstock." Sometimes his friends came down to see him, and spend a while in suppers and amusements as much like town as possible. Sometimes he gibed and jested at the country people; sometimes he acted a part there as well as at Court. He composed impromptus on the parish clerk at a village near by as he had composed them on the King or Lady Castlemaine.

> Sternhold and Hopkins had great qualms,
> When they translated David's Psalms,
>   To make the heart full glad:
> But had it been poor David's fate,
> To hear thee sing, and them translate,
>   By Jove, 'twould have drove him mad.

Stories of his disguises lingered in the neighbourhood for generations; two have been preserved. The first tells how one day he went out into the lanes dressed as a tinker, and made his way to the village of Burford, where he had been at the Grammar School. He called out for pots and pans to mend. The villagers brought them. The tinker, instead of mending them, gave himself vast amusement by knocking out the bottoms. There was a hubbub; the tinker was seized and thrust into the stocks. There he prevailed upon one of the observers to take a note, or at least an order of some kind, to Adderbury, and in good time arrived my lord's carriage with its state of four horses. He was hastily released, entered the carriage, and drove home—presently to send new ironmongery to the villagers. Those whose lives brought them within Lord Rochester's scope had to expect inconvenience; fortunately, in the lower ranks of society, they were sometimes recompensed. A certain trudging beggar had this experience. He one day met a fellow of the art who asked him where he was going. He answered that he was on his way to the Earl of Rochester's, but without much hope, for he had heard that Lord Rochester never gave anything to anyone. The second beggar offered to show him the way; together they came amicably to Adderbury. At the house the wretched creature, slipping round to the servants' quarters, found his comrade calling to the servants to seize him. Under those wild orders he was clutched, carried to a huge barrel of beer, and thrust into it, the Earl threatening him with exuberant blows every time his head appeared over the barrel top. My lord tired at last; the beggar was pulled out, given a meal and clothes, and sent off, with counsel not again to say in any road or inn of that district that my Lord Rochester was ungenerous.

Could he have lost himself he would not have

been. But generosity, though an easy indulgence, is not an easy virtue. My lord kicked his heels in the air, a little despitefully sometimes, and if there were anyone—King, duchess, poet, or beggar—to be tripped up in the antic, so much the higher he kicked his heels.

CHAPTER VIII

THE WAY OF SENSATION

MANKIND was the same everywhere; the follies of village tramps and parish clerks were no less amusing than those of kings' mistresses and kings' ministers. Philosophy compelled Lord Rochester to admit so much, and his natural buoyancy enabled him to admit it. But even a philosopher may have personal preferences, and a saint, at a pinch, prefer apples to pears. As material for life and satire Rochester preferred the follies of Whitehall. As an actor, he was most at home in the part of himself at Court; as a poet, he could give a sharper turn to his verse with the names of his courtly friends.

In pursuit of rough material it is said that he established at one time a system. When the night guards were set in the courtyards of the palace, there stood among the sentries one whom no officer stationed and no trumpet relieved. He wore his red coat; he carried his musket; he made his paces, keeping his watch under the moon and the torches. The moon was a little fallen from her high estate at this time; she was no more a "queen and goddess, chaste and fair," nothing much more now than a convenience or a nuisance. Once she had lit Lorenzo or Titania; now she had to be content to reveal to the fellow in the red coat what he was set to learn; over the forest of man's large imagination she might still romantically shine, alternate to the strange sun of George Fox; by implication, she was there when, almost in these years, Milton spoke of her at Chalfont "hid in her vacant interlunar cave." But that Miltonic moon had not much to do with the Duchess's maids of honour or with others, such as the Dutch prince William, afterwards King of England, who tried to get in at their windows, or with his suite or that of his brother of England.

"The sentinel stars set their watch in the sky." The sentry below stood or marched, and about him the night commerce of King Charles's Court went on. He turned and counterturned; sometimes he remarked faces that he knew; he saw doors open, and visitors made welcome. When, by morning, the stars had withdrawn, so had this other sentry. He went off to the lodgings of the Earl of Rochester. The Earl received and heard him, heard who had visited whom, and what intrigues of the day were confirmed or contradicted by the industry of the night. Then the footman—he was no more—was dismissed. Through a winter—one or more—this went on. "By this means Lord Rochester made many discoveries. And when he was well furnished with material, he used to retire into the country for a month or two to write libels."

It does not seem likely that the Court were aware of Lord Rochester's secret service, or that, to name no others, the King himself would have endured it. The report comes from Dr. Burnet, who (if it is true) may have had it from Rochester himself. In itself it is not unlikely; the connotation of the word "gentlemanly" was quite different in 1670 from that of our day. Rochester owed no dues of honour to any but his few friends—Henry Savile, or Buckingham, or Etherege, or Sedley. His hand and his tongue were against the rest of them. He made for himself his law and his morals; there was about him an energy. In a poem, "To a Lady that accused him of Inconstancy," a declamation in defence of "the flying moment," he wrote:

> No Glorious Thing was ever made to stay,
> My Blazing Star but visits, and away.

By a similar cometary voyage he rounded the Court, thrilled and thwarted by sensations, and plunged into the depth of poetic space at Woodstock with the vapours of rumour that gathered round him, and again returned.

From 1669 to 1677 he followed this quickening ellipse, though the unmilitary sentinel is only one sign of it. His path was marked by excitement and extravagance. So far as one can guess, by the few dates we have, this sweep of energy reached its wildest scope about the years 1675 and 1676. He had abandoned himself to that movement from the first. In 1670 it is known that he belonged to a society called the "Ballers." It had existed for some years, certainly since 1668, for then on 30th May,[1] Pepys had fallen into the company of young Killigrew, who had recently returned from France, but was still in disgrace at Court. He was not so desirable to Charles's awareness of sense and nonsense as his noble friend. Killigrew and his wild company carried Pepys off to supper, "in an arbour." Joseph Harris, the actor, was with them, and amid their "mad talk" the little man heard of the origin of the society; of the society itself he had heard before. He heard of meetings of young blades and prostitutes, of nude dames, and,

[1] He saw *Philaster*, by Beaumont and Fletcher, on the same day, at the King's Playhouse, and exquisitely remembered how once as a boy he was to have acted Arethusa, and had learnt the part.

as he rather sweetly euphemises it, of "all the roguish things in the world." He listened to the talk, half admiring, half revolting, but content, with that immense interest of his, to remark how all kinds of men lived. By 1670 Rochester was a leader of the society; unfortunately he was out of town when a conflict occurred between them and the Revenue officers. He had gone down to Woodstock for the baptismal ceremony by which his son, Charles Wilmot, new born, was to be new born in grace, and the flesh as well as the world and the devil were to be forsworn on his behalf. The proxies, in this case, seem to have been the Lord Buckhurst and Sir Charles Sedley, a sufficiently remarkable pair of covenanting Christians. Henry Savile, brother of the great Lord Halifax, wrote to excuse his own absence. He said he hoped to serve on the next occasion, which he thought would be soon, "y^r L^p staying much with y^r Lady." It is a pleasant phrase, though Henry Savile's hopes were dashed: there were no more children. The reason was perhaps not unconnected with the second half of Savile's letter, in which he alluded to "a leather instrument" which Rochester had carried down into the country. A box containing a number of these, imported from France, had been seized at the Customs, and the contents burnt. Savile and Sedley (newly returned from the christening) descended twice into the City in attempts to prevent the holocaust, but in vain. He summoned the Earl to bring his aid. "Pray consider whether it is fitt for you to bee blowing of coales in the country when there is a revenge due to the ashes of these martyrs." The battle failed, however; in 1672 an Act was passed definitely prohibiting such imports, and Rochester could do no more than contribute to English literature a poem in ballad style, which sang the "virtuous abilities" of the stranger, devastated the ladies of the Court with allusions, and wished ill to all "Citizen Fops" who had been concerned in the burning. The "poor benefit of a bewildering minute" had a vivid place in the awareness of my lord's poetic genius. It is in the mere admiration of that genius that we must admit it was poetically aware of what, in the contrasting line of Mr. T. S. Eliot, has been, with a larger but inclusive scope, called "the infirm glory of the positive hour." It was precisely the "infirm glory" and "the poor benefit" of which my lord's angry contempt was contendingly aware.

Occasionally the benefit was impoverished and the glory weakened after a more actual manner than the merely emotional. In December 1668 a story against Lord Rochester ran through the

Court. Pepys, on the second of the month, came to Whitehall towards the end of a noteworthy day.[1] He wanted to speak to the Duke of York, and made gradual way through the press to where the royalties were. As he came up he heard the King's voice. Charles was telling his circle of Rochester's ill-luck. The Earl had pursued some amorous adventure—probably into the City—and had, at its conclusion, found his clothes gone. Investigation discovered them at last, hidden in a feather-bed—discovered the clothes, but not the gold that had been with the clothes. The minute had been more bewildering than had altogether been expected, and Charles was laughing at the tale—" the silly discourse of the King," said Pepys, a little uncharitable towards Charles's particular pleasures, considering the fervour of his own pleasure in his coach earlier in the day.

Once also it is said—and it is said it was the cause of one of his banishments—Rochester involved the King himself in a not quite similar

---

[1] It is only fair to him to record it yet again. "Abroad with my wife, the first time that ever I rode in my own coach, which do make my heart rejoice, and praise God, and pray him to bless it to me, and continue it." Afterwards he had seen a "pretty good play." But he came to the Court on Navy business. Pepys took his own poor benefit for what it was, desired no metaphysical power behind it, and simply, and Shakespeareanly, enjoyed it.

incident. It was at Newmarket. Charles was bored and allowed the Earl to carry him off to some place of " low " amusement. When he had provided entertainment for his master, Rochester proceeded to entertain himself by means of his master. Unnoticed he removed the King's watch ; he removed the King's money ; the King's ring he could not manage to remove. He withdrew, delicately and secretly, from the company and the house. Presently Charles, again satiated, determined to withdraw, and looked round for his companion. He was told that his companion was already gone ; when he proposed to follow, he was asked for payment. At first amused, he discovered suddenly that he could neither pay nor (consequently) leave. He became angry. He did not wish to make himself known ; the proprietress took him for one of the Court gentlemen who would be easily free with their own money when they had it, but when they had not would as easily make free with other people's. She grew verbosely termagant. The King offered her his ring. She distrusted the ring. The stones were large and ostentatious. One of the first of the moderns, she believed ostentation must be insincere ; she suspected the stones of being false. There was a long wrangle. At last it was agreed they should send for a jeweller, and get him to estimate the ring's value. In the middle of the night they sent, while the King waited. Presently the messenger returned. The jeweller came with him, his curiosity excited by the high value of the stones. He was introduced into the room; he saw the tall figure, the swarthy ugly face, and immediately knew them. He fell on his knees, humbly proffering the ring back to its owner. Around him the proprietress and her people were startled into alarmed dismay. They too fell on their knees, exclaiming, entreating. The King laughed, turned their prayers and apologies aside, asked for another bottle on the ring's security, and returned in due course to his lodgings. But for a while afterwards the Earl of Rochester was excluded from Court.

Of the date of this incident we have no record; the ideal pattern of biography would find room for it near the 1668 adventure, and see in it a small retaliation for the King's laughter in the mode of the social comedy of the time. The pattern would be further agreeably satisfied by that early date because it would then be free to observe by the years 1675–6 an increasing destructiveness in my lord's sensations—slight perhaps, but definite. In default of contrary evidence, and with a timorousness belonging to such biographical temerity, it may be permitted to fix the pattern so, and so to contemplate those later years. In 1675, the year when he was made Keeper of the King's Hawks, there was the destruction of the dial and the adventure with Villiers; in 1676 the adventure of Epsom and the climax of disguise; in 1676 also there was a presentation of a kind of idealized Rochester to the world by Sir George Etherege; in 1677 the energy of the actual Rochester began to turn in on itself, to revolt and mature.

The incident of the destruction of the astronomical dials is a prelude. Aubrey recounts:

"The dials . . . in the garden at Whitehall . . . were one night, anno Dni. 167–(4ª, as I take it), broken all to pieces (for they were of glass spheres) by the earl of Rochester, lord Buckhurst, Fleetwood Shephard, etc., comeing in from their revells. 'What!' said the earl of Rochester, 'doest thou stand here to . . . time?' Dash they fell to worke. Ther was a watchman alwayes stood there to secure it."

Rochester was largely concerned with sensation. The Duke of Buckingham was almost wholly concerned with sensation. He was more eccentric than Rochester, because he had a less fixed desire. So far as he had wit, it was mundane, and not, like Rochester's, metaphysical. He was never converted ; and never to be converted—never to turn from oneself to anything at all beside oneself—is to have a markedly limited nature. A catholic nature is always capable of conversion. In spite of their profound difference, they were courtiers together, though Villiers took a direct interest in politics and Rochester did not. Villiers was used by the King, and betrayed him. Rochester, so far as we can see, permitted himself neither amusement ; he was content with merely saying what at the moment he thought.

He said it this year in a poem called *The Restauration, or the History of Insipids* ; in which the King was attacked not merely for his private behaviour but for his public policy.

> Chaste, Pious, Prudent, C—— the Second,
>   The Miracle of thy Restauration,
> May like to that of Quails be reckon'd
>   Rain'd on the *Israelitish* Nation ;
> The wish'd for Blessing from Heav'n sent,
> Became their Curse and Punishment.
>
> . . . . .
>
> His Father's Foes he doth reward,
>   Preserving those that cutt off's Head :
> Old Cavaliers the Crown's best Guard,
>   He lets them starve for want of Bread.
> Never was any King endow'd
> With so much Grace and Gratitude.

Considering the income of £1000 that Rochester was drawing as a Gentleman of the Bedchamber, and the various posts that he held, Charles may well have felt that gracelessness and ingratitude were not royal prerogatives. The poem, however, had no more liking or regard for the Families in the Lords and Commons:

> A Parliament of Knaves and Scots,
>   Members by name, you must not mention,
> He keeps in pay, and buys their Votes,
>   Here with a Place, there with a Pension.
> When to give money he can't cologue 'um,
> He doth with scorn prorogue, prorogue 'um.
>
> But they did long since by too much giving,
>   Undid, betray'd, and sold the Nation;
> Making their Memberships a Living,
>   Better than e're was Sequestration.
> God give thee C—— a Resolution
> To damn the Knaves by Dissolution.

It grew extremely anti-York and anti-France, and ended with an anti-monarchical revolutionary fling. At other times, however, other flings. He borrowed an earlier anonymous poem, and improved it, in order to comment on the growth of the Power of the Families:

> THE COMMON'S PETITION TO KING CHARLES II. AND
>   THE KING'S ANSWER
>
>   In all Humanity we crave,
>   Our Sovereign may be our Slave;
>   And humbly beg, that he may be
>   Betray'd by us most Loyally.

> But if he please once to lay down
> His Scepter, Dignity, and Crown,
> We'll make him for the Time to come,
> The greatest Prince in Christendom.

> *The King's Answer*
> Charles, *at this Time having no Need,*
> *Thanks you as much as if he did.*

For the *History of Insipids,* or for some other reason, the Earl of Rochester was in disgrace; so also was the Duke of Buckingham. The King did not wish to see them. They left the Court together, and rode out on the road to Newmarket. Some little distance from the town, at a place called Six Mile Bottom, they stopped at an inn, which was to let. Rochester rose to the opportunity; he and his companion took charge. They adopted other names, whether their own were guessed or not; in turn they played the landlord. The inn, under their government, became a centre of festivity. Feasts were made and all the neighbourhood invited. Wine was extravagantly poured for the masculine guests, and love made as extravagantly to the feminine. Over some days there was a riot of freedom. It could be but brief, for the neighbourhood would become suspicious, and even, in the guardianship of its ladies, hostile; besides, the King might pass at any moment. Among the ladies, however, Rochester had seen one with whom he either desired to press his acquaintance, or had been hindered by her husband from beginning it. She lived not far off ; the husband was old, vigilant, and reported to be miserly. The story rises into exact Restoration comedy. The Duke of Buckingham, taking his turn at playing host, invited the old gentleman to supper, and in a generous spirit of brotherly love devoted the time to making him drunk. The Lord Rochester, disguising himself in the clothes of a country girl, went off to the house. Finding some difficulty in getting past the lady's sister-in-law who acted as guardian, he permitted himself to be overcome by exhaustion and to faint on the threshold. The door was thrown open ; the lady came on the scene, and was kind. She had the poor girl brought in and put to bed. At a convenient moment, when the old lady was out of the way or incapable (asleep, it is said, after drinking a drugged bottle of cordials which the poor girl had been carrying), the great actor returned to his favourite part and revealed himself. The lady remained kind.

The story than takes a darker and more doubtful turn. After some hours of pleasure, my lord and the lady determined to escape together. She collected what money she could find ; they fled, and on their way heard the husband coming home. Concealed by the wayside, they waited till he had passed ; then they hurried on to the inn. While the two gentlemen there admired, welcomed, and flattered the fair fugitive, the old man, discovering what had happened, hanged himself. Very soon after, the King on his way to Newmarket came to the inn, and was received by the lordly keepers. He laughed, pardoned their transgressions, including the old man's death, and took them back into his favour. When they had concluded their amusement with the lady, they sent her on to London " to find another husband."

It is so proper a story that one a little mistrusts it. But there is nothing absolutely unlikely about it. Rochester would not have regarded himself as responsible for the death of the old man, nor would the King, nor, for that matter, would strict Christian theology. One would like not to believe it, but one can do no more than remain doubtful. The way of sensation passes through strange and hideous places, and Rochester, when all has been said, was a Restoration sensationalist. He had been destructive in his art, and tales of destruction began to attach themselves to his person. Something dark followed him ; gossip becomes macabre. He dances, for a year, as it were, on the edge of graves, whether there are bodies within them or not. The edge even of a deeper Pit shows, the Pit of destruction and self-destructive madness to which the way of sensation leads. The light and lovely verse, the light and obscene verse, the driving satire, have in them a realism of death.

He translated, or was to translate, a few lines from Seneca :

> Dead, we become the Lumber of the World,
> And to that Mass of Matter shall be swept,
> Where things destroy'd, with things unborn are kept ;

After death—had not Windham taught him as much in that unattained vision ?—there was nothing. He would not claim as much in his philosophy, but the doubt rose into a climax in his verse. Hell and the fool Fiend

> With his grim grissly Dog that keeps the Door,
> Are senseless Stories, idle Tales,
> Dreams, Whimseys, and no more.

Let us gather roses, let us seize the moment, let us plunge into " Love's fantastick Stories."

> Fool—is not sleep the Image of pale Death ?
> There's time for rest, when Fate hath stopt your breath.

Let us enjoy.

> His Wisdom did his Happiness destroy,
> Aiming to know the World he should enjoy.

But, alas! to aim to enjoy the world one should know seems no more satisfactory. If there were only some way of knowing and enjoying at once! There is perhaps some single perfection which is to be found neither in direct enjoyment nor in indirect knowledge, for whichever man chooses he is aware of some loss. A lover beholding lovers finds himself contemplating some curious experiment of delight which he desires to study with a metaphysical zeal; he sees beauty in pure action, and when from that busy contemplation he returns to his own beloved and his own passion, still sometimes a wistful doubt lingers in him. Yet to study alone is so cold a business, and how can one study a thing whose essence is missed unless indeed, existing in the spectator, it turns him from spectator to actor by the violence of its power within him? So perhaps poetry arises, and in the search of its " stormy pathless world " the discoverer finds for a moment at least a vision of the knowledge and the enjoyment at once. But if the poetry is to do that, it must be of the highest kind; neither the lesser romantic nor the lesser classic is quite sufficient. Rochester, in whom both strove, strove to rise to the union. In life, as in art, he desired to know and to enjoy, and death and imperfect fruition haunted him.

It is unfortunate, certainly, as Gilbert Burnet

was afterwards to point out to him, that our own enjoyment should so often be inconsistent with that of others. The discipline which teaches us to derive joy from others' joy was, in practice, a little beyond the Earl's study. In July 1676—on the 22nd, a Sunday—he, Sir George Etherege, and a Captain Burgess, had gone down to Epsom. The incident there was recorded by Charles Hatton in a letter:

"Mr Downs is dead. Y^e Ld Rochester doth abscond, and soe doth Etheridge, and Capt Bridges who occasioned ye riot Sunday sennight. They were tossing some fidlers in a blanket for refusing to play, and a barber, upon ye noise, going to see what ye matter, they seized upon him, and, to free himself from them, he offered to carry them to ye handsomest woman in Epsom, and directed them to the constables house, who demanding what they came for, they told him a wh . . ., and, he refusing to let them in, they broke open his doores and broke his head, and beate him very severely. At last, he made his escape, called his watch, and Etheridge made a submissive oration to them and soe far appeased them that ye constable dismissed his watch. But presently after, ye Ld Rochester drew upon ye constable. Mr Downs, to prevent his pass, seized on him, ye constable cryed out murther, and, the watch returning, one came behind Mr Downs and with a sprittle staff cleft his scull. Y^e Ld Rochester and ye rest run away, and Downs, having noe sword, snatched up a sticke and striking at them, they run him into ye side wth a half-pike, and soe bruised his arme y^t he wase never able to stirr it after. He hath given his estate, wch wase 1500 per annum, to his sister, and is reported ye Ld Shrewsberry is to marry her. But some say his estate was entayled on a kinsman of his."

It was in the same year, and may have been in connexion with his retirement from the Court consequent upon this death, that the most notorious of his disguises took place. He had made himself familiar before now with the City that stretched away from Whitehall to the Tower. The City and the Court were chained together by more and closer links than when, in the days of the King's grandfather, James I., there lay between them only the huge fetter of the houses of the great lords. The social and political connexion was also closer. Degree was still kept, but money, though it did not smell, was talking more and more loudly. In another few years the Lord Shaftesbury was to raise the frenzy of the rabble and the foolishness of the richer men against the Crown. City society was intensely aware of Court society. The virtuous women envied the King's Duchesses their dresses; the vicious envied them their lovers. The Great Plague and the Great Fire had not purged the houses of prostitutes and quacks. Henry Savile had been defeated there in the War of the Leather Implements; the Lord Rochester's raids were more lonely and more victorious.

Anthony Hamilton relates an earlier story similar to this of 1676, but his date—not that he gives one—is impossible. Either Rochester tried the trick twice, or someone else had done it, or Hamilton heard some vague tale of the second effort. Rochester was said to have been left surprisingly long in one of his banishments by the King. He came up from the country, determined to have something to do with the Court, and being debarred thence went to the City. There, in a grave dress, with a grave face, he inserted himself. He made friends with the Mammon of a different kind of unrighteousness than his own, and with grave censure deplored his own. He walked among the citizens, and heard their shocked comments on the Court and the Government. He joined in them, and outwent them. The sincerity of his satire at

Whitehall became the insincerity of his sermons in the City. He wondered at the patience of God—as indeed, not being a theologian, he very well might, and in some strange corner of his heart actually did. There was, remotely, in him a perverse tendency to provoke that "Hob-over-the-Wall."[1] He prayed aloud for fire from heaven to consume such abandoned wretches as Rochester, Killigrew, and Sidney! He sighed for horror and shame; citizens, thinking of the Government and the taxes, sighed with him; citizens' wives, thinking of the King, Louise de la Keroualle, and Nell Gwynn, "the Protestant whore," as she called herself, sighed more deeply. They pressed the devout intelligent critic to their dinners and sessions of wine. He endured for a while and fled.

He fled, not to Whitehall, but farther into the City. So far Hamilton, of that dubious early prank; the rest is better authenticated. In 1676, whether or not this prelude were then true, the play was acted. It was a world in which many quack remedies were advertised, both for the body

---

[1] The phrase is from the medieval Townely Mysteries. It is used by Cain when God speaks to him after the murder of Abel. "How now, what is this Hob-over-the-Wall?" And we are still sometimes told of the simple faith of the medieval writers. High art, and hardly simple faith, produced so admirable a description of the omniscience of Deity.

and the soul. Wandering doctors set up their signs, published their claims, and worked—or did not work—their surprising cures. In that very year, 1676, one had appeared in the West End of the town, a Welshman, who proclaimed that he could cure "any wound whatsoever in the bowels or any part, except the heart, in a few hours." "Several pigges, kidds, and chickens," wrote Mr. Christopher Hatton from London to his brother "have, in ye King's presence, been run into ye bowells and through ye head wth knives and hot irons, and cured in a short time by this man's medicines. Should he goe unto ye King of France's army, he wou'd render all ye designs of ye Spanyards and Dutch ineffectuall."

My lord determined to take a turn in this part also. He put on new clothes, he changed his complexion; he took lodgings. He wrote what we should call a prospectus—"Alexander Bendo's Advertisement"—and had it printed as a broadside. It is an admirable piece of work, and should have given the Earl of Rochester a great deal of pleasure in its composition. Some of it ran as follows:

"*To All Gentlemen, Ladies, and Others, whether of City, Town, or Country,*
ALEXANDER BENDO
Wisheth all Health and Prosperity.

"Whereas this Famous *Metropolis* of *England* (and were the Endeavours of its worthy Inhabitants equal to their Power, Merit, and Vertue, I should not stick to denounce it, in a short time, the *Metropolis* of the whole *World*)—Whereas this City (as most Great Ones are) has ever been infested with a numerous Company of such, whose Arrogant Confidence, backing their Ignorance, has enabled them to impose upon the People, either premeditated Cheats, or at best, the palpable, dull, and empty Mistakes of their self-deluded Imaginations in Physick, Chymical, and Galenick, in Astrology, Physiognomy, Palmestry, Mathematicks, Alchymy, and even in Government it self; the last of which, I will not propose to Discourse of, or meddle at all in, since it no ways belongs to my Trade or Vocation, as the rest do; which (thanks to my God) I find much more safe, I think equally Honest, and therefore more Profitable: But as to all the former, they have been so erroneously practis'd by many unlearned Wretches, whom Poverty and Neediness for the most part (if not the restless Itch of Deceiving) has forc'd to straggle and wander in unknown Paths, that even the Professions themselves, though originally the Products of the most Wise Men's Studies and Experiences, and by them, left a wealthy and glorious

Inheritance for Ages to come, seem by this Bastard-Race of Quacks and Cheats, to have been run out of all Wisdom, Learning, Perspicuousness, and Truth, with which they were so plentifully stock'd, and now run into a Repute of meer Mists, Imaginations, Errours, and Deceits, such as in the Management of these idle Professors indeed they were.

"You will therefore (I hope) *Gentlemen, Ladies,* and *Others,* deem it but just; that I, who for some Years have with all Faithfulness and Assiduity, courted these Arts, and received such signal Favours from them; that they have admitted me to the happy and full enjoyment of themselves, and trusted me with their greatest Secrets; shou'd with an Earnestness and Concern more than ordinary, take their parts against those impudent Fops, whose saucy, impertinent Addresses and Pretensions have brought such Scandal upon their most immaculate Honours and Reputations. . . .

"First, I will, by the leave of God, perfectly cure that *Labes Brittanica,* or Grand *English* Disease, the *Scurvy,* and that with such ease to my *Patient,* that he shall not be sensible of the least Inconvenience whilst I steal his Distemper from him; I know there are many who treat this Disease with *Mercury, Antimony, Spirits,* and

Salts, being dangerous Remedies, in which I shall meddle very little, and with great Caution, but by more secure, gentle, and less fallible Medicines, together with the Observation of some few Rules in Diet, perfectly cure the *Patient,* having freed him from all the Symptoms, as looseness of the Teeth, Scorbutick Spots, want of Appetite, pains and lassitude in the Limbs and Joints, especially the Legs. And, to say truth, there are few Distempers in this Nation that are not, or at least proceed not, originally from the Scurvy; which were it well rooted out (as I make not question to do it of all those who shall come into my hands) there would not be heard of so many Gouts, Aches, Dropsies, and Consumptions: Nay, ev'n those thick and slimy Humors which generate Stones in the Kidneys, and Bladder, are for the most part Offsprings of the Scurvy. . . .

"I will not here make a Catalogue of Diseases and Distempers; it behoves a *Physician,* I am sure, to understand them all: But if any one come to me (as I think there are very few have escaped my *Practice*) I shall not be ashamed to own to my *Patient,* where I find my self to seek, and at least he shall be secure with me from having Experiments tried upon him: a priviledge he can never hope to enjoy, either in the hands of the Grand Doctors of the Court and Town, or in those of the lesser Quacks and Mountebanks. It is thought fit, that I assure you of great Secresie as well as Care in Diseases, where it is requisite, whether Venereal, or other ; as some peculiar to Women, the Green-Sickness, Weaknesses, Inflammations, or Obstructions in the Stomach, Reins, Liver, Spleen, &c. (For I would put no Word in my Bill that bears any unclean sound ; it is enough that I make my self understood ; I have seen Physicians Bills as bawdy as *Aretine's Dialogues* ; which no Man that walks warily before God can approve of.) But I cure all Suffocations in those Parts producing Fits of the Mother, Convulsions, Nocturnal Inquietudes, and other strange Accidents, not fit to be set down here, perswading young Women very often that their *Hearts* are like to break for Love, when God knows the Distemper lies far enough from that place. . . .

"As to Astrological Predictions, Physiognomy, Divination by Dreams, and otherwise (Palmestry I have not faith in, because there can be no reason be alledg'd for it) my own Experience has convinc'd me more of their considerable Effects, and marvellous Operations, chiefly in the directions of future Proceedings, to the avoiding of Dangers that threaten, and laying hold of Advantages that might offer themselves.

"I say, my own Practice has convinc'd me more than all the Sage and Wise Writings, extant of those Matters: For I might say this for my self (did it not look like Ostentation) that I have very seldom failed in my Predictions, and often been very serviceable in my Advice; how far I am capable in this way, I am sure is not fit to be delivered in Print. . . .

"Nor will I be ashamed to set down here, my Willingness to practise rare Secrets (though somewhat collateral to my Profession) for the Help, Conservation, and Augmentation of Beauty and Comeliness: A thing created at first by God, Chiefly for the Glory of his own Name, and then for the better establishment of mutual Love between Man and Woman: God had bestowed on Man the Power of Strength and Wisdom, and thereby rendred Woman liable to the Subjection of his absolute Will: it seem'd but requisite, that she should be indued likewise in recompence, with some Quality, that might beget in him admiration of her, and so inforce his Tenderness and Love. . . .

"The knowledge of these Secrets, I gathered in my Travels abroad (where I have spent my time ever since I was Fifteen Years Old, to this my Nine-and-Twentieth Year) in *France* and *Italy*: Those that have travelled in *Italy* will tell you to what a Miracle Art does there assist Nature in the preservation of Beauty; how Women of Forty bear the same Countenance with those of Fifteen; Ages are no way distinguished by Faces, whereas here in *England*, look a Horse in the Mouth, and a Woman in the Face, you presently know both their Ages to a Year. I will therefore give you such Remedies, that without destroying your Complexion (as most of your Paints and Dawbings do), shall render them purely fair, clearing and preserving them from all Spots, Freckles, Heats, and Pimples, any Marks of the Small-Pox, or any other accidental ones, so the Face be not seam'd or scarr'd.

"I will also preserve and cleanse your Teeth, white and round as Pearls, fastning them that are loose; your Gums shall be kept entire and red as Corral, your Lips of the same colour, and soft as you could wish your lawful Kisses. . . .

"I will besides (if it be desired) take away from their Fatness who have over-much, and add Flesh to those that want it, without the least detriment to their Constitutions.

"Now should *Galen* himself look out of his Grave, and tell me these were Bawbles below the Profession of a Physician, I would boldly answer him, that I take more Glory in preserving God's Image in its unblemish'd Beauty, upon one good Face, than I should do in patching up all the decay'd Carkasses in the World.

"They that will do me the favour to come to me, shall be sure from Three of the Clock in the Afternoon, till Eight at Night, at my Lodgings in *Tower-Street*, next door to the sign of the *Black Swan*, at a *Goldsmith*'s House, to find
Their Humble Servant,
ALEXANDER BENDO."

In Tower Street, next to the sign of the Black Swan, the wise Doctor dispensed his remedies. The City heard of him, and after the City the Court. Maids of the Maids came searching out the Black Swan and the goldsmith's shop, and went back with wild tales of truth. It seems a little astonishing that Rochester omitted palmistry from his sciences. Palmistry, one would have thought, would have been his surest method and experiment. Perhaps the Advertisement counterfeited there in order to give the true man his proper chance. " There can be no reason alledg'd for " many entertaining habits, and the Italian doctor may have had to resort to it, if stars, features, and dreams were something unrevealing, to discover—each case an exception—" the direction of future Proceedings."

After the maids the Maids. The rumour of

the wise doctor flew up to the higher places of the Court. Another delicious excitement presented itself to the more daring ladies. The adventure of the journey and the adventure of the interview mingled together. Anything might happen and anything be said. On some former escapade Frances Jennings, disguised as an orange-girl, had been pushed down in the crush at the Play-House, and her rank only discovered by her stockings. Anthony Hamilton describes how, on that same day, Miss Jennings and her companion Miss Price were accosted by Mr. Henry Brouncker, the traitor of the Duke of York's naval victory, who either mistook or pretended to mistake Miss Jennings for a bawd and Miss Price for a prostitute, and desired to hire the prostitute for a seraglio which he kept in the country. The interviews which Lord Rochester held were hidden from the chroniclers. After a while he tired of them, and of the Black Swan, and the goldsmith's shop; he left them and fled again to Whitehall or Woodstock, to take up once more his own proper part in the interminable play. The play, it seemed more and more certain, was without a climax. By whatever chance it had been staged, the original dramatist, no abler than Settle or Crowne, at once hastier than Shadwell and slower than Wycherley, had omitted from his inartistic effort merely the plot.

During these years, 1676 and 1677, the King made a habit of holding little supper parties with a few friends. They took place, sometimes in the rooms of the Duchess of Portsmouth, sometimes in Nell Gwynn's, sometimes in Chiffinch's; and were generally attended by Harry Killigrew, Henry Savile, Buckhurst, Mulgrave, one or two more, and Rochester "when in town." He sat lighter perhaps than some of the others even to the King's good graces. Once the poet, Edmund Waller, was present in Rochester's own rooms; in a letter ascribed to him an account is given:

"Grammont once told *Rochester*, that if he could by any means divest himself of one half of his Wit, the other half would make him the most agreeable man in the World. This Observation of the Count's did not strike me much when I heard it, but I have often marked the Propriety of it since. Last night I supped at Lord R——'s with a select party—on such Occasions he is not ambitious of shining—He is rather pleasant than arch—He is, comparatively, reserved; but you find something in that Restraint, which is more agreeable than the utmost Exertion of Talents in others. The Reserve of *Rochester* gives you the idea of a copious River, that fills its channel, and seems as if it could easily overflow its Banks, but is unwilling to spoil the Beauty and Verdure of the Plains. The most perfect Good-humour was supported through the whole Evening, nor was it the least disturbed, when, unexpectedly, towards the End of it, the King came in. . . . Something has vexed him, said *Rochester*; he never does me this Honour but when he is in an ill Humour. The following Dialogue, or something very like it, ensued :

The King : How the D——l have I got here ? The Knaves have sold every Cloak in the Wardrobe.

Rochester : Those Knaves are Fools. That is a Part of Dress which, for their own sakes, your Majesty ought never to be without.

The King : Pshaw !—I'm vexed.

Rochester : I'm glad of it. I hate still life. Your Majesty is never so entertaining as when——

The King : Ridiculous !—I believe the *English* are the most untractable People upon earth.

Rochester : I most humbly beg your Majesty's Pardon, if I presume, in that Respect——

The King : You would find them so, if you were in my Place, and obliged to govern.

Rochester : Were I in your Majesty's Place, I would not govern at all.

The King : How then ?

Rochester : I would send for my good Lord of *Rochester*, and command him to govern.

The King : Oh ! but the singular Modesty of that Nobleman !

Rochester : He would certainly conform himself to your Majesty's bright Example. How gloriously would the two grand social Virtues flourish under his Auspices.

The King : O *prisca Fides*. What can those be ?

Rochester : The Love of Wine and Women.

The King : God bless your Majesty !

Rochester : These Attachments keep the World in good Humour, and, therefore, I say they are social Virtues—Let the Bishop of *Salisbury* deny it if he can.

The King : He died last Night. Have you a mind to succeed him ?

Rochester : On Condition that I shall neither be called upon to preach on the Thirtieth of *January* [the anniversary of Charles I.'s execution], nor on the twenty-ninth of May [the anniversary of Charles II.'s Restoration].

The King : Those conditions are curious. You object to the first, I suppose, because it would be a melancholy Subject; but the other——

Rochester : Would be a melancholy subject, too.

The King : That is too much——

Rochester : Nay, I only mean that the Business would be a little too grave for the Day. Nothing but the Indulgence of the two grand social Virtues could be a proper Testimony of my Joy upon that Occasion.

The King : Rochester, thou art the happiest Fellow in my Dominions. Let me perish, if I do not envy thee thy Impudence.

It is in some such Strain of Conversation generally that this Prince passes off his Chagrin, and he never suffers his Dignity to stand in the way of his Humour. If Happiness be the end of Wisdom, I know not who has a right to censure his Conduct."

The Earl of Rochester satirized his fellow-actors; he satirized himself also and the play. "He was," wrote Horace Walpole later, "a man whom the Muses were fond to inspire and ashamed to avow." In some of those poems from which the blushing Muses turned, there is nevertheless more than the mere cause of their blush. "Imperfect enjoyment," "imperfect fruition," "the maim'd debauchee "—under such titles he celebrated the deplorable mischances that attend on the physical activities of the sexes. They are admirably realistic things in themselves, but they have another reference. Consciously or not —and probably not—they relate, in conjunction with others of his poems and with his activities, to that pattern of life itself which lies beneath sex. He lamented the waste it seemed to promise; he longed for fruition. " Give me more vigour, less activity." The moment of fruition, the very flying moment itself, was apt, even in sex itself, to slip by. And as it there mockingly escaped, so the great unguessed romantic fruition of life seemed to escape also.

>   Eager Desires confound my first intent !
>   O what envious gods conspire
>   To snatch his power, yet leave him the desire !
>   Labouring Man, who toils himself in vain,
>   Eagerly grasping what creates his pain.

Besides the deceit of sensation, what was there ? Reason ? " an ignis fatuus of the mind,"

>   that makes a Mite
>   Think he's the image of the Infinite.
>   .   .   .   .   .
>   So charming Ointments make an old Witch fly,
>   And bear a cripled Carkass through the Sky.
>   'Tis this exalted Pow'r whose business lies
>   In Nonsense and Impossibilities.

Reason had only one business : so to govern sense as to invigorate desire. Once he had been willing to give it a larger scope. He had desired a miracle ; it seemed miracles did not happen. Yet, almost hopeless, almost despairing, almost unaware of his own persistence, the Lord Rochester, hurling himself down the Way of Sensation, went on looking for a miracle.

CHAPTER IX

THE WAY OF ARGUMENT

IN the year 1678 Rochester was thirty-one. He was beginning to suffer from increasing attacks of illness. His search for a miracle had been discouraged by his failure to find one, and by interim enjoyment of extravagant sensations. In those sensations my lord had been vividly aware of himself, but he was weary of being aware of himself. He was approaching the way of compromise ; he was growing ready to be reconciled to time. The mere energetic pursuit of the moment displeased his spirit, and yet his spirit had found neither the completeness of eternity—that is to say, God—nor any credible method of approaching eternity. He did not, in fact, believe that eternity could be approached by man. Yet, at the close of his youth, his spirit began to feel it must settle its energies towards some steady labour. He was alive, whether he liked it or not ; he had power, which he did like. Vaguely, his mind began to feel towards the serious occupations of time. He was becoming aware of the world again, but now through all the narrower channels of closing youth.

The first signs of it are in 1677. He began to object to extravagant gossip. Lies which were used for artistic purposes, especially by Lord Rochester, were one thing. He defended his own use of them in his satires : " The lies in these libels came often in as ornaments that could not be spared without spoiling the beauty of the Poem." Lies, however, especially lies about Lord Rochester, which were merely repeated in chatter at supper, were less tolerable.

He had always been then (as he has been since) a mark for gossip and scandal. There is a reference to something of the sort in 1671, when one of his correspondents wrote to him from London : " Now, my Lord, as to a concerne of your owne. Fate has taken care to vindicate your proceeding with Foster, whoe is discovered to bee a damsell of low degree, and very fit for the latter part of your treatment, noe northerne lass but a mere dresser at Hazard's scoole, her uncle a wyght that wields the puissant spiggot at Kensington, debaucht by Mr Buttler a gentleman of the cloak and gallow-shoe, an order of knighthood very fatall to maydenhead."

It seems as if Mr. Butler's misdeeds had been put to Rochester's account, and as if Miss Foster had been attempting to " put it over " the Earl.

On 4th June 1677, he had been at supper with a company. In the same tavern, in another room, had been a more violent company, which had closed in one of the not unusual murderous affrays ; the victim was one Du Puis, a French cook. He had returned some rude answer to a gentleman named Floyd, and Mr. Floyd had naturally stabbed him. When next day the tale of the deed went about the town, it was heightened by the substitution of Rochester's name for Floyd's. It was, everyone heard and everyone said, " the mad Earl " who had bloodily struck down the insolent cook. Others had been in his company ; they were not involved. The story threatened to reach the provinces. " He desired me," wrote Henry Savile to his brother, the great Lord Halifax, " to write to you to stop that report from going northward, for he says if it once gets as far as York, the truth will not be believed under two or three years."

It is by no means impossible that it was Halifax rather than the north whom Rochester wished to correct. The two were not unsympathetic. Halifax had a high opinion of the Earl, and the Earl was intimate with Henry Savile. In the political mêlée of the age, Halifax stood for the moderate and loyal Whigs. He belonged to the Families, but he was faithful to the Crown, up to the last struggle between the Crown and the Families—but that was eleven years later. Both he and Rochester were aristocrats of the high kind. Their republicanism was, as was natural, a class republicanism, which Halifax finally assisted to establish for a century; and that aristocratic republicanism was checked by their personal sympathy with Charles. Even Mr. Belloc has allowed that Halifax was—oddly enough—" never caught taking money," and though Rochester was sometimes in difficulties, no scandal of purse or land has attached itself to his name. Halifax was then a man of forty-four, and the correspondence with William of Orange had not begun.

It was to Henry Savile that, from about this time, most of Rochester's letters were written. In the September of 1677 he wrote, this time from the country, to deny another tale. The masquerades of King Charles's Court were alternated sometimes by extremes of the opposite kind. Sir Charles Sedley especially seems to have been given to stripping off the conventional lendings of civilization. In 1663 he had " shown his nakedness " in, and preached " a mountebank sermon " from, the balcony of a tavern in

Bow Street, after which he in the same state and place drank the King's health. Buckhurst had been with him, and had been driven in with him by brickbats thrown by the moral crowd. The court of justice before which he was brought found "there was no law against it," but the Lord Chief Justice said it was owing to Sedley and such wretches that God's anger hung over the State, and bound him over in £5000. Five years afterwards Pepys, to whom we owe this story, heard another. He had gone with his friend, Pierce, a surgeon, to Tyburn to see a hanging (two women and one man), but they were too late. On the way Pierce told stories of the wickedness of the Court, and how Sedley and Buckhurst, who had run by night through the streets, again offensively exposed, had had an affray with the watch, and been confined; how the King had taken their parts, and the Chief Justice was holding the constable to answer for his action.

Similar gossip, in 1677, reached London of Rochester. He and his friends were said to have run about Woodstock Park naked, "on the Sabbath." Henry Savile, hearing it, wrote to the Earl, warning him of it, and saying "you alone speak truth of yourself." Rochester, with a slight mockery, answered: "For the *hideous*

Deportment, which you have heard of, concerning *running naked*, so much is true, that we went into the River *somewhat late in the Year*, and had a *frisk* for forty yards in the Meadow, *to dry ourselves*. I will appeal to the *King* and the *D*. if *they* had not done *as much* ; nay, my *Lord Chancellor*, and the *Archbishops both*, when they were *Schoolboys* ; and, at *those Years*, I have heard the one *declaim'd like* Cicero, *the other preach'd like* St. Austin : *Prudenter Persons*, I conclude, *they* were, *ev'n in hanging sleeves*, than any of the *flashy Fry* (of which I must own *Myself the most unsolid*) can hope to appear, *ev'n in their ripest Manhood*."

He proceeded to remind Savile of partial nudisms in which they had both taken part at Woodstock in 1676 " round Rosamond's fair Fountain," comparing Savile to folio volumes and himself and two other friends to quartos. As for the invitation by which his friend had begged him to come to London and help entertain the Dutch train of William of Orange, " if *God in mercy* has made 'em *hush* and *melancholly*, do not you *rouse* their *sleeping mirth*, to make the Town *mourn*." And he ended by sending, with the letter, a musician who would amuse the King. " May he *dream pleasantly, wake joyfully, love safely and tenderly, live long and happily*."

He wished good things to Charles and Savile, but he himself was sick and depressed. "I am *almost* BLIND, *utterly* LAME, and scarce within the reasonable hopes of ever seeing LONDON *again*."

He was in the country and ill when his last child was born—but not at Woodstock. Elizabeth Barry gave birth to a daughter in 1677. The news came to the Earl in a letter from Savile. "The greatest news I can send you from hence is that the King told me last night that your Lordship has a daughter born by the body of Mrs. Barry of which I give your Honour Joy. I doubt she does not lie in much state, for a friend and protectress of hers in the Mall was much lamenting her poverty very lately, not without some gentle reflections on your lordship's want, either of generosity or bowels towards a lady who did not refuse you the full enjoyment of her charms."

He wrote to his mistress :

"MADAM,

Your safe *Delivery* has deliver'd me too from *Fears* for your sake, which were, I'll promise you, as *burthensom* to me, as your *Great-belly* cou'd be to you. Every thing has fallen out to my wish, for you are out of *Danger*, and the

Child is of the *soft Sex* I love. Shortly my *Hopes* are to *see* you, and in a little while after to *look* on you with all your *Beauty* about you. Pray let no body but yourself *open* the *Box* I sent you ; I did not know, but that in Lying-inn you might have use of those *Trifles* ; *sick*, and in *Bed*, as I am, I cou'd come at no *more* of 'em ; but if you find 'em, or whatever is in my *power* of *use*, to your Service, let me *know* it."

It seems, therefore, that the moment had prolonged itself here. Rochester was the last person to maintain a love affair beyond his own wishes, except in a courtesy which would hardly have dictated that letter. The child—her name was also Elizabeth, he called her Betty—lived to the age of fourteen. The Earl left her in his will an annuity of £40, "to the payment of which I bind the mannour of Sutton-Mallet."

It is said that he began to read Law, Constitutional History, and the Journals of Parliament ; history he had studied, and now studied English History. He had asked Savile to let him know if the Parliament was likely to sit, "for the Peers of *England* being grown out of late Years very considerable in the Government, I wou'd make one at the Session. *Livy* and Sickness has a little inclin'd me to Policy," and though then he had not taken this inclination very seriously, by that same November in which William of Orange, by now very steadfastly inclined to high policy, married the Mary Stuart for whom Crowne had written *Calisto*, Rochester either allowed or encouraged himself to be elected Alderman for Taunton.

He had not, however, much time to be useful to Taunton. In the next year, 1678, Savile was sent to Paris, and Rochester felt the separation. He had not many friends. " I ever thought you *an Extraordinary Man*, and must now think you such a *Friend*, who, being a *Courtier*, as *you* are, can *love a man* whom it is *the great Mode to hate*." His illness continually returned : " I'm taking pains not to die, without knowing how to live on, when I have brought it about. But most human Affairs [are] carried on at same nonsensical rate, which makes me (who am now grown superstitious) think it a Fault to laugh at the Monkey we have here, when I compare his Condition with Mankind." Petulant, hungry, and good-tempered, he dragged through the year.

Before it was ended England was swept by a great outburst. Sensation was enjoyed, indulged, and encouraged. While the grand metaphysical romantic lay ill at Woodstock or, a little recovered,

THE WAY OF ARGUMENT 215

came up to London ; while he played still with satire or speculation ; while he half resolved and half refused to be respectable, another young man, two years younger than himself, came back to London from the Continent. He was one who, unlike Rochester, sought no justification for his desires beyond their mere existence. He did not wait for a cue ; he spoke his line, and the world of England answered him. He ranted, and the world responded with shuddering enjoyment of its sensations. He would have been a romantic, had he believed in his cause ; since he did not believe, he was but a pseudo-romantic. If the world which he so violently moved had been self-abandoned to a cause, that also might have been romantic ; as it desired only its self-preservation, it also was but pseudo-romantic. The name of that large young man, bulbous, strident, altogether abominable, was Titus Oates.

Neither he nor the movement he initiated, and men as evil but less blatant than he encouraged, had any direct relation to Rochester, nor much indirect. Only at one moment does the Earl appear. When, in the slow and dreadful course of the Popish Plot during the months, among the uproars and executions, the Peers of England sent five of their Roman Catholic members to the Tower, and the Commons had resolved that "there has been and still is a damnable and hellish plot," they proceeded to attack the Succession. The first Exclusion Bill, by which the rights of the Duke of York to the Throne were cut off, was introduced in May 1679. The Earl of Rochester rose to speak against it. It does not read—what we have of it—like a very effective speech; it was mild, but definite. It declared that there was a loyal party which "will think themselves bound by their oath of allegiance and Duty, to pay Obedience to the Duke, if ever he should come to be King, which must occasion a civil war." It did not very certainly suggest whether Rochester did or did not belong to that party. Probably he did not know himself. But it is pleasant to think that, since he spoke, he spoke so, and that, in the midst of a corrupt frenzy besides which even the search for sensation appears civilized, he was separated from George Villiers, Duke of Buckingham. George Villiers was a leader in both search and frenzy. One cannot blame him; simply, he was that kind of man.

It was the other side of the grand romantic search, the peril that accompanies extravagance and enthusiasm, the spectre of horror that walks behind George Fox and John Wesley, and many of the mystics and the saints. The almost-Augustan coolness of Charles II. knew it for a lie, but he would not or could not interfere. He played high and secretly against it ; he took a fierce revenge on the party that encouraged it ; he turned a snarl against it when it approached the Queen. For the rest, he signed the death-warrants. He was fighting for his brother and the monarchy. Halifax and a few others stood by him. Even the Favourites were divided. The Duchess of Portsmouth, "a brave, hectoring lady," denounced the Duke of Monmouth, the great popular figure ; Nell Gwynn pleaded for him—"the King bid her be quiet." Charles kept his mind secret from all ; in August he was taken ill ; they thought him dying, but in September he recovered.

The Earl of Rochester saw an altered country and Court. Without, as within, the old delights had faded. About him men went mad. Even if he had agreed with them, he would not go mad. "The general heads," he wrote to Savile, "under which *this whole island* may be consider'd, are *Spies, Beggars,* and *Rebels,* the *Transpositions* and *Mixtures* of *these* make *an agreeable variety ; Punie Fools,* and *Cautious Knaves* are bred out of 'em, and set off wonderfully ; tho' of this latter sort, we have *fewer now* than *ever*, *Hypocrisie* being the only Vice in *decay* amongst us, *few men* here dissemble their being Rascals ; and no Woman *disowns being a Whore.*" He went on mockingly to tell a story against Dr. Oates, and give an account of the hubbub between the Duchess of Portsmouth and Lord Mulgrave. But there was a cloud over him.

The romantic spirit, in fact, was entering upon that unpleasant state of growing pains which true romanticism, though it dislikes, can hardly avoid, and of this no more than of his earlier passion could his adequate mind find a convincing explanation. A conviction of sin ruled in him. But he did not know it as that, for the reader of Hobbes could hardly speak of sin ; the courtier of Charles had no clear notion of it ; and Rochester's own ethics did not accuse him of it. A dark night, and monstrous visions, closed in ; why ? Was this also part of mere "ridiculous being," or was there a particular cause ? It went sometimes, but it returned. He had no very particular evil on his mind, other than the nature of the whole world, which sensation might momentarily obliterate but could not wholly destroy. In matters of morality the King and he agreed. Charles held, anyhow for purposes of public profession and action, that

THE WAY OF ARGUMENT

appetites were free, and that God would never damn a man for allowing himself a little pleasure; that to be wicked and design mischief—like the perpetrators of the Popish Plot—is the only thing that God hates. He told Dr. Gilbert Burnet so, "and," added Burnet, "he has said to me often that he was sure he was not guilty of that." Even Charles II. tended to think God was much of a muchness with him. Injury to others deliberately intended and carried through—this was the great, the only, fault. "He had formed an odd idea of the goodness of God in his mind." "Odd" is hardly the word; it is not an exalted, but hardly a degenerate, conception of God that He should willingly permit His creatures all such delight as hurts neither themselves nor others.

"Malice," wrote the King, "is a much greater sin than a poor frailty of nature." Dante had admitted as much long before; he did not stop there. The fact is but a beginning; it is hardly a sufficient map of the heavenly world. George Fox would not have reached his hollow tree, much less emerged from it into the "paradise of God," had he been content with so moderate a maxim. It is indeed almost an encouragement to the "imperfect fruition" of joy, and any romantic explorer into spiritual things who is content with it thwarts the purpose of his journey before it is begun. The necessary thing for him is not the comfort of knowing that there is a much greater sin, but the discomfort of believing that there is a much greater good.

The King's " minister of pleasure," however, with a much more romantic heart than the King's, yet held the King's doctrine. His two maxims of morality, he said, were " to do nothing to the hurt of any other or that might prejudice his own health " ; these safeguarded, he thought " all pleasure might be indulged." The definition raises, as Burnet saw, other difficulties. When exactly does hurt to any other begin ? When the Duke of Buckingham, having seduced the Countess of Shrewsbury, killed her husband in a duel, presumably he injured Shrewsbury, even in the sense of Charles Stuart and John Wilmot. But would he have done any injury if there had been no duel ? Must the sensations of the Duke and the Countess be limited by the Earl's emotions ? Obviously, no, said Anthony Hamilton ; obviously, yes, said Gilbert Burnet. At what point does " injury " commence ?—and who determines it ?

Rochester was no Buckingham. As things go in this world, he thought he had committed very little injury to others. Like another young man, he had kept the commandments—or almost. He had killed no one; he had robbed no one; and if he had ever committed adultery it had never been without the consent of his partner. He did not regard the husbands, if any, of his paramours as being injured. He was an English gentleman of his time, and he had in that matter all the points of view and prejudices of an English gentleman of his time. " In England they are astonished at any man who would be so uncivil as to be jealous of his wife," wrote Hamilton; it seemed to him the English were in this more courteously civilized than most of Europe. It may at least be noted that this also is a morality, and in certain conditions difficult. Even if broken, however, it did not promise to cause such dark presages in the soul, if there was a soul. The Earl was not conscious of having broken this morality, nor was he convinced of the existence of any other. He was willing to endure his darkness, but he still at the bottom of his heart desired that it should be justified and significant. The " divinations of spirit " which had haunted him in the *Revenge*; the " stormy pathless world " which he had discerned in poetry; the passion which despised those others who thought it " below wit " to admire anything; the greater passion which called love "the only joy for which poor we are made," and cried of his companions:

> To an exact perfection they have brought
> The action love; the passion is forgot;

all these, now almost defeated, were gathered in a last effort to question his heart's oracular thunder.

There were the philosophers, with whom, failing any better solution, he was inclined to agree, though it fretted him almost as much to agree with the popular view of life as it had done to allow the popular view of Dryden to agree with his. Probably there was only one popular view all through his life with which my lord was inclined to agree, and that was the view that the Earl of Rochester was a unique and astonishing being. The temptation was sometimes subtle, and he fell; when it was obvious, his intelligence and his laughter restrained him. There were the clergy; Lord Rochester had no high opinion of the clergy. He seems to have held the common idea that the clergy ought to be better men than the rest of us—an idea as natural as it is mistaken. It is a pseudo-romantic view, unconsciously aimed at our self-preservation from grace by the vicarious sacrifice of others. In general, the clergy seemed to Rochester either worldlings or mystery-mongers, and he could not believe that the mystery with which he desired to be concerned was given into the dispensation of a group of (on the whole) rather unintelligent and self-seeking persons. It is not very severely to blame the clergy whom he had met to say that their search for advancement and Rochester's search for abandonment crossed, and found no sincere common tongue. The dialects of the romantic forest are many and difficult. He was profane and sincere; they were pious and solemn. Besides, so many silly people agreed with them.

At certain moments in this period, a little earlier or a little later, two figures of his youth reappear—Dr. Whitehall and Mr. Giffard. Dr. Whitehall produced a present for the young Charles, Lord Wilmot. In 1677 Dr. Whitehall edited and published a quarto volume with a title written in three languages—brief Greek, long Latin, and longer English—*Being an Epigrammatical Explanation of the Most Remarkable Stories throughout the Old and New Testament after each Sculpture or Cut.* "It must be noted," wrote Anthony Wood, "that the author had brought from Holland as many cuts of the Old and New Testament that cost him 14*l*. Each cut he caused to be neatly pasted in the middle of a large quarto paper, on which, before, was printed a running title at the top, and six English verses at the bottom to explain the cut or picture. Which being so done, in twelve copies only, he caused each to be richly bound, and afterwards presented a very fair copy to the King, and the rest mostly to persons of quality : of which number was Charles, son and heir of John Wilmot, earl of Rochester, for whom he pretended 'twas chiefly compos'd." The volume can still be seen in the British Museum.

At a later date, probably in 1679, the earlier tutor appeared—almost as if Time were leading the Earl back through the acquaintances of his youth, to the country of his first, and now of his second, birth. Mr. Giffard came to call. As he told the story afterwards : " Says his lordship, ' Mr. Giffard, I wonder you will not come and visit me oftner. I have a great respect for you, and I should be extremely glad of your frequent conversation.' Says Mr. Giffard (who could say any thing to him), ' My lord, I am a clergyman. Your lordship has a very ill character of being a debauched man, and an atheist, and 'twill not look well in me to keep company with your lordship as long as this character lasts, and as long as you continue this course of life.' ' Mr. Giffard,' says my lord, ' I have been guilty of extravagances, but I will assure you I am no atheist'; with other words to the same purpose."

Mr. Giffard's caution may have robbed him of the chance of a great victory, except that it is not generally by the teachers of our childhood that our maturity is disturbed. Another of that cloud of clergymen which begins to loom around the Earl's path, said later that the Earl of Rochester was " a great man every way—a great wit, a great scholar, a great poet, a great sinner, a great penitent." Mr. Giffard, all unknowing, had declined to have a hand in his penitence; that was left to a stronger mind. In the entanglement of his emotions Lord Rochester heard once more of Burnet.

Once or twice in their lives their paths had drawn near one another's, and something about Burnet had attracted Rochester—his sincerity, his metaphysics, or, more likely, the power of his personality. Here, at least, was somebody who could talk, who could argue, and whose energy was equal almost to Rochester's own. Energy is only caught by energy. It was intellectual energy that had made Hobbes Rochester's master; it was passionate energy that had made Elizabeth Barry Rochester's mistress. He knew the stories told of this clergyman. Charles had once remarked that he thought Burnet would be willing to be hanged in order to have the happiness to make a speech on the scaffold, "but I will order drums so that he shall not be heard." When this came to Burnet's ears he answered, "When it comes to that, I will put my speech in such hands that the world shall see it if they cannot hear it." That very year the first volume of Burnet's *History of the Reformation* had been published, and he had been thanked by the House of Commons. The midst of the Popish Plot was an admirable time to choose, but authors are sometimes fortunate; it was an accident. Rochester, talking of it to the King, and in allusion to Charles's dislike of Burnet, said he wondered "why he would use a writer of history ill, for such people can avenge themselves." The King, wrote Burnet, answered: "I durst say nothing while he was alive, [and] when he was dead he should not be the worse for what I said." Retorts were thus easy between the two of them.

It was, however, a more serious incident that brought Burnet to Rochester's mind now. Burnet's account is that he had been summoned to the death-bed of "one with whom Wilmot, Earl of Rochester, had an ill concern." It is thought it may have been a certain Mrs. Roberts, once a favourite of the King. Gossip declared she had deserted the King for his servant, had been in turn deserted by the servant, and had made the best of her plight by hurrying to throw herself at the King's feet when she saw him go by, one morning while she was dressing, to implore pardon, and to promise constancy. The King received her and was reconciled. If indeed it were Mrs. Roberts, then Rochester heard how Burnet, going from the death-bed, had written to Charles, exhorting him to penitence; how the King had read the letter twice, and burnt it, and been angry. He heard also that Burnet had behaved nobly to the dying woman, " being neither too easy nor too hard," speaking of sin and of salvation, and between recollection of the one and assurance of the other assisting her to her peace. Burnet, it might be, could intelligibly interpret the secret monitions; Burnet perhaps could convince his reason and satisfy his passion; Burnet might know of some wonder neither as easy as the laughter of the Court nor as hard as the outcries of the Ranters. In October 1679 he caused a friend to signify to the cleric that the Earl of Rochester was desirous to see him. So, but more hastily, five years later the King, in his last hours, was to permit the calling of a minister of another Church. Burnet obeyed; he came to the Earl's apartments, and the Earl willingly received him. They conversed. Through a whole winter, almost every week, they conversed.

We have only Burnet's account, which is, no doubt, as truthful as it could be. Unfortunately Burnet's piety, though he assures us it gives the matter of Rochester's part in the discussion, suppressed the manner. " I saw he made an ill use of his wit . . . [I have not given] all the excursions of his wit. . . . He slurred the gravest things." Alas! Rochester's slur was likely to be exactly one of the gravest things, the mark of the mind, the direction of the heart, the presage and divination of the soul. " He was under no such decay as either darkened or weakened his understanding." His melancholy for a while had lifted; he flung himself freely and eagerly into the discussions. His talk, as always, danced to the music of his fancy. It was in the music that part of the truth lay, and it was the music that Burnet suppressed. Rochester was grave after another fashion than Burnet understood, or the nation or the age to which Burnet belonged. His gravity was wild; his seriousness danced, and his intellect. His style half belonged to another age. Dryden himself complained that Donne affected the metaphysics " . . . in his amorous verse where nature only should reign," and if Dryden failed to understand the mode of Donne, how could Burnet follow the mode of Rochester ? He who thought St. Teresa " melancholick " thought Rochester frivolous. Yet they conversed, across a gulf, but recognizably. They saw not only that gulf, but another, the gulf of the self and of the universe. One lured by it, the other unafraid of it ; one shooting burning arrows of doubt, the other sinking flaming lamps of reason ; all that winter, while the Plot around them roared and flagged, and the King fought and watched and waited for his hour, they conversed.

Burnet's record of the conversations, besides omitting the music of the mad Earl's thought, allows much less talk to the Earl than to himself. It is likely that there he is truthful, though there we could have done with less truth. They began with that three-quarters of life which is conduct, and the rules that should govern it. Rochester admitted the necessity of rules ; he admitted the need of a moral law and a moral life. As he had pleaded years ago to the King, so in effect he admitted now, that his own inadvertence, ignorance of the law, and passion, had brought him into imprisonment, but now chiefly a spiritual, though ill-health and ill-report helped to bar the doors. Deducing the general from the particular, he concluded that morality was needed for the preservation of such good things as health and friendship. He proposed so to change his life as to ensure their presence. Philosophy would direct and assist him. There was no need to introduce the idea of God; against him, if he existed, there could hardly be any offence in the casual follies of existence.

Burnet shook his head. Philosophy would hardly serve. There was neither common agreement upon it nor natural efficacy in it. Besides, it knew of no exact rule of limitation. Its only safe doctrine was the Stoic. That could work, by checking all passion, and therefore by lessening friendship, and the chief pleasures of life, which arise from friendship. It is a mark of the hour that those two metaphysicians chose, as the great good of life, friendship, and not romantic love. Rochester had failed in that; Burnet had never found it. Their age confirmed their choice; the calm strength of the Augustan stability is already at hand.

Rochester answered by repeating his two maxims: do not hurt yourself; do not injure others. Under those conditions all was permitted. Were the mere natural appetites to be roughly refused? was wine not to be drunk? were women not to be enjoyed?

Burnet asked, justly, how injury to others was to be measured; less justly, he added that to corrupt a man's wife or daughter was comparable to killing or robbing him. He attacked vagrant lusts with eloquence, pointing other misfortunes or faults to which they led—failure of intelligence, increase of profanity, increase of hypocrisy, extravagant expense, false dealings. When my lord seemed to assent, he went on to urge that mere conventional or legal morality had no final effect. More was needed—the mind must take delight in virtue; the spirit must indeed be regenerate.

"This," Rochester said, "sounds remarkably like canting or enthusiasm. I have no notion at all of that." Philosophy . . . philosophy and reason. . . . "As the mind becomes conversant with their dictates, it will find it easier to obey."

Proudly meek, Burnet returned scorn for scorn; Rochester found himself mocked. What did all philosophy amount to? "*Video meliora proboque; deteriora sequor*"—this is the end of all your reason. It is God only who assists, God only by whom the evil impressions of the spirit are disengaged and cast off, God only who reforms all.

"Say rather a heat in nature," the Earl

answered. It had, though perhaps he did not say so, always in his experience been but a heat in nature which had promised so much and failed to bear fruit. Where was the need of God? It is the strong diversion of the thoughts that gives a seeming victory. If one could turn heartily to working a problem in Euclid or writing a copy of verses, the effect would be the same.

"Yes, indeed," Burnet said, "if a mere diversion of thought were all that the crying upon God effected; but what of the utter freedom from ill, the easiness and delight in holiness, the true love of good?" Man had two guides, he added, experience and reason. Experience without reason might be only perfervid fancy; reason without experience might have frigid operation; by the two together man found his satisfaction.

"No; it is but fancy," the Earl answered, and clung to that dogma through much talk. The continued refusal of his once-desired experiences refused now to allow Burnet to prove the possibility of their truth. Those who could believe, he said, were happy; their thoughts had a rest and a centre. But for himself there was no such rest, no power that dealt directly and mightily with man. His thoughts found no centre; the circumference which philosophy provided must be their limitation and their accustomed stay.

Nevertheless, now that the great name, which in different ways meant so much to both of them, had been pronounced in that room of controversy, the disputants paused upon it. They had come from the laws of conduct to something more; to what? Burnet had spoken of crying upon God, of prayer. The Earl frankly scorned the notion. God, yes, perhaps; he did not deny. A supreme and remote creative energy; a lofty, unperturbed, inhuman power—that, yes; but what has that to do with us? "It is the heat of fanciful men that they should pretend to love God"; again he used the defensive word. Better that we should not think much of Him, since our notions were so low, our hopes so poor, as to believe Him weak enough to be overcome by importunity or perverse enough to bestow rewards and punishments, "the one too high for us to attain by our slight services, the other too extreme to be inflicted for sin." What! shall we attribute to God affections of love or hate? as absurd to do so as it is presumptuous to talk of loving Him! "There ought to be no other religious worship but a general celebration of that Being in some short hymn; the rest is the invention of priests." Pope was to write some such hymn; Shelley, in more aerial music, to denounce priests. Before them both, my lord sneered and adored at once; shall men pretend to hold the secret of incensing or appeasing God?

It was the talk of the Deists, sincere, and in a sense rational enough, but utterly inadequate. Burnet, in the face of a lofty humility as arrogant as his own, attempted to show its inadequacy. He did what could be done; he had, however, to take the jump necessary to all apologists, and he did that in one pathetic sentence—a sentence so pathetic that it seems impossible a man as intelligent as Burnet could either have spoken or written it. But he says he did. "I told him . . . if the order of the universe persuaded him to think there was a God, he must at the same time conceive Him to be both wise and good, as well as powerful, since these all appeared equally in the creation." To which all one can say, with one intonation or another, is merely "Good God!" Burnet himself appears to have been uneasy, for he added that God's "wisdom and goodness had ways of exerting themselves that were far beyond our notions or measures." From so doubtful a defence and so necessary a modification, he returned to the central thing in which they were both more interested—the heart of man, especially of Lord Rochester. Certainly truth and goodness, mercy and love, raised no passion or perturbation in deity; that they should in us was due to our want of power or skill. Certainly our worship could not add to the happiness or "fond pleasure" of deity; its purpose was not so at all. It was meant only to arouse meditations in *us*, to incite apprehensions of God in *us*, to deepen their roots and strengthen their influence in *us*. It is for *our* profit that ritual and awful form are meant. We can "love" God in the attributes of His infinite perfection. And as for the corruption of the priesthood, why, corruption occurs in everything, in law, in medicine. "Mountebanks," added Dr. Burnet, "corrupt physic."

Rochester ignored the gentle gibe, or replied to it by one of those extravagances of wit that Burnet omitted. He allowed that reform, of the self or of the world, was very difficult. He had claimed that his satires were meant for that purpose, and in the complexity of his motives it may be allowed as an element. As in the later work of the Augustans, the refusal of another world caused the mind sometimes to turn back, with increased passion, to the refining and purifying of this. It felt what experience it had with the greater keenness, almost with a rapture of keenness, because it refused other and greater experiences. The knife with which Pope flayed Addison, for his egotistical second-rateness, was sharpened on the stone which he, in common with other builders, refused : the stone of the corner of the metaphysicals. Rochester had not so much refused it, for Hobbes and the rest had done that, as failed to recognize it as a stone fit for foundations. He had sharpened his knife on it, nevertheless. His passion for the spirit enraged him the more against such unspiritual lives in the world as could not keep even the fineness of the world.

Satire is rarely accepted by its victims ; he had not reformed the world. He allowed, in this interlude, that frequent impressions of God, such as Burnet required the penitent heart to impose upon itself, might work strongly to that end. But he could not or would not allow that those impressions could be vivid, or at least that there was any rational way of making them so. A man cannot help his belief ; he can believe only as he can. Nor did he think much of any future life, recognized by and recognizing this life. The soul may be immortal, but not so as to retain any remembrance or figure of its past. Rather, he thought, in some other state it began a new course. So far from our present mode of experience he removed all other, retaliating upon the supernatural the decision which had been imposed upon his mind.

It was Burnet's turn, upon hearing these high speculations, to cry out "Mere fancy!" Up the ascending spirals of the mind they pursued each other, each accusing the other of aerial inventions. Rochester accused Burnet of forcing the evidence; Burnet accused Rochester of ignoring it. In order to prove his points of responsibility and judgment, he turned again to interior witnesses; he spoke (rather rashly) of the impressions of joy or horror sustained by the good and the wicked as they drew towards death. The Earl answered that these were due to early impressions, sealed by education. Since there must be some explanation of his own fear and longing, he was content that they should be attributed to his own education—to Lady Anne, Sir Ralph Verney, Mr. Giffard, and the rest. He admitted no sacred knowledge in the heart; rather, he returned again to his former point—a man can believe only what he can. Those who could believe this other doctrine were happy. Moved by that desire for a centre and for repose, he exclaimed, "I would give all I am master of to believe." Burnet challenged his sinful life as the cause of his incapacity. Rochester did not altogether deny it; it might be so. He was exactly rational, but it was the first gate opened in his wall. Presently the powers that govern change were to breach the wall itself. He said that "after the doings of some things he felt great and severe challenges within himself." But, he urged, these came after acts which his adversary might not consider very terrible sins; he had felt no such challenges after acts Burnet might more strongly disapprove. Here perhaps the doctor missed the right answer. He declared that Rochester's "ill life" had destroyed his spiritual sense of proportion. "A feverish man cannot judge of taste." The true answer seems to be that the proportions of sin and of beauty differ in every man. Rochester must deal with his own challenges first.

They passed to revealed religion, on which, unfortunately, we possess only a ha'porth of Rochester to a monstrous deal of Burnet. The Earl had many objections. He objected to the style of the Bible, which seemed to him often "incoherent." He objected to the rite of circumcision among the Jews; "it seemed unsuitable to the Divine Nature." So Burnet, omitting any extravagant mirth. The real objection lay deeper. "He could not comprehend how God should reveal His secrets to mankind." His remote Deism forbade him; he was consistent. He was consistent more deeply. He had made innocent demands, and they had been refused. Passion and pride were both angered. God, his passion cried, did not reveal His secrets to men; for God, his pride added, had not revealed them to the Earl of Rochester.

Dr. Burnet's answer to this, his defence of the Scriptures and the Church, occupies forty-two pages out of the ninety which are given to these discussions. The details are unimportant. They did not convince the Earl. He was left in the end with two main objections, one metaphysical, one moral. They were, in fact, the same two with which he had started, but they were compact and pointed. "He excepted to the belief in mysteries." "It is not in a man's power to believe that which he cannot comprehend; and of which he can have no notion." That was the first objection. The second was equally important. "The restraining a man from the use of women, except one in the way of marriage, and denying the remedy of divorce, he thought unreasonable impositions on the freedom of mankind." Dr. Burnet fought hard. He assured the Earl that men had a property in their wives and daughters which it was unjust to ignore; my lord did not much seem to think so. Burnet added that under a state of polygamy women were miserable, jealous, and barbarously used; our Saviour, he said, had realized this, and determined to make life more tolerable for them. The Earl might have accused him of a fault in argument. Polygamy may be part of the barbarous usage; it is not clearly responsible for it. As for our Saviour, only in the high sense of mystical redemption can He so far be generally said to have made life more tolerable for anybody. Burnet, with some dim realization of this, pointed out the celestial rewards that are promised to those who performed their proper conditions. " We are sure the terms are difficult," Rochester said dryly; " we are not so sure of the rewards."

At the end, therefore, it was still mystery and marriage which stood in the way of their agreement. The Earl desired still to believe what he could and to woo where he chose. The doctor desired to enlarge his creed and limit his concupiscence. He failed, yet his failure was victorious. Through that winter Rochester's interior longings had strengthened and shaped themselves. He was determined to correct his life. Philosophy would help him. So perhaps it might have done, but it never had a chance. Not in vain had Burnet beaten with the hammer of the gospel on the stone. The Earl had, as a rational builder, rejected the stone over which he had stumbled. It fell from heaven, as had once been prophesied, and ground him to powder.

CHAPTER X

THE WAY OF CONVERSION

THE winter had passed; it was April 1680. The blood-lust of fear aroused by Oates and his like was a little satiated. Its managers felt it failing under their hands. "Man," Rochester had written,

> Inhumanely, his fellows Life betrays,
> With voluntary Pains, works his Distress;
> Not through Necessity, but Wantonness.

It might have applied to Buckingham, as the line that follows might have applied to many of the respectable citizens—"Wretched Man is still in Arms for Fear."

> Wrong'd shall he live, insulted o'er, opprest,
> Who dares be less a Villain than the rest.

London was full of the sodden content of the persecutors. Summer was approaching. The Earl of Rochester had determined to reform. Gilbert Burnet, still dubious of his noble penitent's perseverance under the inadequate guiding of philosophy, was left behind in London ; the Earl set out for the country.

It may have been then, or a little later, that he composed a poem which was given the title of *Rochester's Farewell, 1680*. It is a superb effort of invective—more than two hundred lines of denunciation of Mulgrave, Monmouth, Buckingham, the Duchess Mazarin, the Duchess of Portsmouth, and many lesser personages. The King was left comparatively scatheless, and the Duke of York was even praised as " the best of masters." The general crowd, it may be noted, were, at the moment, generally hostile to the Duke. It has a fine opening :

> Tir'd with the noysom Follies of the Age,
> And weary of my part, I quit the Stage ;
> For who in Life's dull Farce a part would bear,
> Where Rogues, Whores, Bawds, all the head Actors are ?
> Long I with charitable Malice strove,
> Lashing the Court, those Vermin to remove,
> But thriving Vice under the Rod still grew,
> As aged Letchers whipp'd, their Lust renew ;
> Yet though my Life hath unsuccessfull been,
> (For who can this *Augæan* Stable clean)
> My gen'rous end I will pursue in Death,
> And at Mankind rail with my parting breath.

Somewhere about 1680 also Rochester took a hand in the great literary game of rewriting the Elizabethans which was so widespread through this and the next century.[1] He had implied a rebuke of Dryden's own criticism of them:

> But does not Dryden find ev'n Johnson dull?
> *Fletcher* and *Beaumont*, uncorrect and full
> Of lewd Lines as he calls 'em? Shake-speare's stile
> Stiff and affected; to his own the while,
> Allowing all the justness that his Pride
> So arrogantly had to these denied?

A rash reader might comment in turn that presumably Rochester found Beaumont and Fletcher not quite full enough of lewd lines. Certainly his *Valentinian* has a good deal more sex complication in it than the original. But it would be unfair to Rochester to say he only increased the lewdness; he seems to have wished to increase the virtue. The plot of the original play deals with the Emperor Valentinian's rape of Lucina, the noble wife of his general Maximus, and with the

---

[1] There exists another play, entitled *Sodom*. Of *Sodom* it is enough to believe, with Anthony Wood, that it was "father'd upon the Earl (as most of this kind were, right or wrong, which came out at any time, after he had once obtained the name of an excellent smooth, but most lewd poet)."

A similar adoption of the Earl's name is referred to in a letter from Buckingham. "My noble friends at Court have now resolved, as the most politick notions they can goe upon, to ly most abominably of your Lordship and mee in order to which they have brought in a new Treasonable Lampoone of which your Lordship is to be the author."

friendship between Maximus and Aecius. Aecius is killed by the Emperor's command, on the pretext of conspiracy, though in fact he is a loyalist of the most extreme kind. The last act struggles on through the death of the Emperor (poisoned by another injured subject), the succession of Maximus, and his poisoning in turn by the Emperor's widow. It involves a change in the character of Maximus which is left extremely unconvincing, and a concluding speech by the imperial poisoner which is entirely untrue.

All this Rochester cut, and (from the point of view of shapeliness) did well. In compensation he enlarged the part dealing with the imperial temptation of Lucina, and gave Valentinian a little homosexuality to make him more interesting. This is not the place for a full examination of the two versions, were it at all worth while; which is doubtful, seeing that neither has in it much of the real poetic energy. It will be sufficient to remark a few suggestive points of my lord's rewriting.

There is, first of all, an increased megalomania in the Emperor. He was tyrannical and sacrosanct in the original, but in Rochester he is much more aware of himself so. He sends panders to persuade Lucina, but when they return he tells them—

> Had your poisonous flatteries prevailed
> Upon her Chastity I so admire,
> A Virtue that adds Fury to my Flames!
> Dogs had devour'd ere this your carcasses.

He must have her, but he must have her " chaste and uncorrupted." In the same union of opposites, the two maids of Lucina are sketched in, as one virtuous and the other lascivious, and their dialogue ends with the renewed contrast that cheating Wit—

> though the Fancy with vile shows it please
> Yet wants a power to satisfy the mind.

Finally, there was introduced by Rochester a kind of lyric ode by Maximus on his misery, which though printed as blank verse was composed in stanzas:

> Gods! would you be ador'd for being good,
> Or only fear'd for proving mischievous?
> How would you have your Mercy understood?
> Who could create a Wretch like *Maximus*,
> Ordain'd tho' guiltless to be infamous?
>
> Supream first Causes! you, whence all things flow,
> Whose infiniteness does each little fill,
> You, who decree each seeming Chance below,
> (So great in Power) were you as good in Will,
> How could you ever have produc'd such ill?

Had your eternal minds been bent to good,
Could humane happiness have prov'd so lame,
Rapine, Revenge, Injustice, thirst of Blood,
Grief, Anguish, Horror, Want, Despair and Shame,
Had never found a Being or a Name.

'Tis therefore less impiety to say,
Evil with you has Coeternity,
Then blindly taking it the other way,
That merciful and of election free,
You did create the mischiefs you foresee.

Valentinian was acted in 1685. The Prologue was spoken by Sarah Cooke, and the noble and chaste Lucina was acted by Elizabeth Barry.

In the country Rochester's health revived. He wanted to go from Woodstock into Somersetshire, and determined to ride thither. On his way he fell ill again. In his weakened state the riding brought on an inflammation of the bladder; he was compelled to abandon his horse and his journey and return by coach to Woodstock. There he lay in considerable danger and extreme pain. His wife was with him; his mother hurried to join him. The doctors gathered round him; so did the clergy.

The winter arguments with Burnet had excited his mind and also his emotions. He was aware—how should he not be?—that many of Burnet's arguments were futile and some foolish. His exhilarated intelligence had proposed to "run 'em down with all the argument and spite in the world." The sentence is only reported from him second-hand, and it seems unlikely that "spite" is the right word. "Spirit" perhaps. He said, or it was said that he said, "he had been arguing with greater vigour against God and religion than ever he had done in his lifetime before." If the winter show was the best fight that the stout champion of Christendom could put up, Lord Rochester felt that all was over but the shouting. He would be the champion of rational religion; he would be the leader of the great Deistic charge. Mystery and priesthood were to be abolished in favour of a humane ethical philosophy, reflecting itself remotely in an unknown God. *À bas l'infame!*

Rational religion reckoned without its nerves, its emotions, its imagination—perhaps its soul. The desire for meaning in death and love, in the universe itself, which had so long haunted the search for sensation, had been no less renewed and excited by Burnet's talk. The God who gave "motions to the soul" drew closer behind the veil of argument and habit. The God who (as Francis Bacon said) "loves to play hide and seek with his creatures" poised in his hiding-place. As the Earl lay in his distress, the "general dark melancholy" that he had known previously changed to "a penetrating cutting sorrow." The double pains incited each other, and before the twin agonies the rational intelligence fled. Right Reason, Lord Rochester had written,

> helps to enjoy,
> Renewing Appetite;

and again:

> Where Action ceases, Thought's impertinent.

Action had ceased now, and Thought was indeed impertinent. An older poet had said that there was never yet philosopher who could endure the toothache patiently. My lord's mind and body burned together.

In this state he lay. The Dowager Countess was with him; she was a Puritan. The Countess was with him; she was a Papist. (In view of everything, one may suppose that she was less strenuously Papist than her mother-in-law Puritan.) The clergy of the district came round. On 26th May, on the Earl's return from the West, the chaplain of the house, the Reverend Robert Parsons, was sent to him. In the circumstances it is a significant name. "The Earl," he said, "showed him extraordinary respects upon the score of mine office." The Earl, whose very chiding of his servants was agreeable to his friends, was the last person, unless angered, to make an obvious inferior feel his inferiority. He permitted the chaplain to read to and exhort him.

Presently the physical ulcer broke. At some close time, the chaplain sat reading by my lord's bed. He had chosen that day the fifty-third chapter of Isaiah, full of the supreme abandonment of Messianic prophecies. My lord, full of pain and cutting sorrow, lay listening. In his own extreme abandonment, conquered by terrible sensations, incapable of making demands upon the universe, there entered into him the tender sweetness of immortal words. The "stormy pathless world" of poetry for which, sometimes selfishly, sometimes unselfishly, he had fought, exquisitely entered into him, and out of that world a unity of emotion. His purpose, suddenly and mightily, was achieved.

Who hath believed our report? and to whom is the arm of the Lord revealed?

For he shall grow up before him as a tender plant, and as a root out of a dry ground; . . .

He is despised and rejected of men; a man of sorrows, and acquainted with grief: . . .

He was wounded for our transgressions, he was bruised for our iniquities: . . .

He was oppressed, and he was afflicted, yet he

THE WAY OF CONVERSION 251

opened not his mouth : he is brought as a lamb . . . as a sheep before her shearers . . . he openeth not his mouth. . . .

In a darkness, in a contradiction, in a covenant with death and a mute ostentation of love, "*he openeth not his mouth.*" John Wilmot had demanded that He should speak, had raged and rated, denied and defied, and He had not—so long He had not—opened His mouth. And now, in the forest of darkness and pain, He appeared, coming in the sound of the august words, to meet which all that belonged in John Wilmot to poetry and death and love rose in a lordly and passionate abandonment. Here was a thing to which no applause of the crowd could disturb fidelity, for after all conversions it remains solitary, a thing in which the union of all opposites was more fantastic than in any riot of mortal thought. Authority—it was his own word—had him ; the world of George Fox had him. He was constrained at last ; he was justified at last. He had been right ; there was romantic passion in the universe. He believed " in his Saviour, as if he had seen Him in the clouds," as indeed he had. The image of a beauty long and madly desired rose in the clouds of that superb rhetoric, and the tide-ways of a vigour that went far deeper than all activities. Here was the glorious drama he had never yet found ; here was the cue for which through his life he had waited. All of the actor in him leapt to the foreordained part.

Who hath believed our report ? " Such wretches as he had opposed it."

He hath no form nor comeliness . . . no beauty that we should desire him—" no fool's coat " such as the vain and foolish delighted in, Castlemaine and Buckingham and himself, and Mulgrave and Mazarin and himself, and the ambition of Monmouth and himself, and the boredom of Charles Stuart, and still, always and chiefly, himself.

He shall see of the travail of his soul, and shall be satisfied ; by his knowledge shall my righteous servant justify many ; for he shall bear their iniquities.

My lord lay in his bed ; power and sweetness took him : " he spoke marvellous things."

He set himself, with a new singleness of heart, but with no less than his old capacity for acting, to play the part appointed him. He had never been so utterly himself. He had taught Elizabeth Barry " to adapt her whole behaviour to the situations of the character." He took his own counsel. He repented ; he adored ; he turned to devotion and piety. He caused himself to receive the Blessed Sacrament with all his family ; it was the great dramatic opening of the new life. He dictated a letter to Burnet, signed it, and bade it be sent at once. It was full of himself—not unnaturally but significantly. He denounced Hobbes and the philosophers—" they have been my ruin," and caused a Bible—a large Bible—to be brought, upon which he laid his hand, saying in rapture, " This is the true philosophy." His family took their parts, with spirits as devoted as his own. His mother wrote letters of mingled thrilling joy and distress to her sister, the Lady St. John, at Battersea. The young Countess did more : she left her own high-road and came to join him on his. Devoutly companionable, as if again, and again perhaps with her consent, she was carried off from the heavy coach in which she sedately rode, she abandoned the Roman profession, and received Communion with her husband. "His lady," wrote one of Sir Ralph Verney's correspondents, " is returned to her first love, the Protestant religion, and on Sunday last received the sacrament with her lord." He went on, that elderly country gentleman, to say that the Earl's restoration to health would give great joy "to us all that love him." Rochester retained, in his weakness and penitence, what he had had in his strength and fantasy, a dominating energy, and also a captivating charm. He imposed power and love on his household and his acquaintance as he had terrified with power and moved with love the courtiers and ladies of Whitehall. Lady Rochester, having turned to God in the absence of her husband, turned now to her husband in the presence of God. Tenderness grew again between them. *La triste heritière* entered into a brief heritage of joy : no less real that it was compelled by the necessity of his sickness. She had for him " a most passionate care and concern."

The rumour of the change got abroad. " The mad Earl " was said to be mad indeed. On one occasion at least he did actually become light-headed at night, and the laughter and language of which his mind was full poured from him. His mother, watching and hearing, heard what she called, " no hurt, only some little *ribble-rabble* which had no hurt in it," and even amid the *ribble-rabble*, whenever he spoke of God, " he spoke well, and with great sense." She and his wife were amazed ; it seemed to them of the nature of miracle. It was not perhaps so astonishing ; my lord's past had never regarded God without great sense, though the kind of sense had changed. But light-headed he had been, and in the opinion of some of his friends, he was not only light-headed but altogether agley.

His mother attributed these tales partly to a "Popish physician," partly to a Mr. Fanshawe. The physician had overheard the Earl conversing with one of his clerical visitors, the chaplain, the minister of the parish, the bishop of the diocese; they all, very properly, waited on him. The Earl, speaking low because of his weakness, used phrases which, half heard, might, his mother thought, sound ridiculous, and, needing someone to blame for the evil reports, she blamed the Roman physician. Certainly the Roman Church, like all other great institutions, and to an extent like Dr. Burnet, has deprecated high emotional crises in religion. It may be that to a cautious medical mind this scene in the Earl's drama seemed more wildly theatrical than it was; especially in view of the reconversion of the Countess.

More definite, however, than the Dowager's suspicions of the doctor was her anger at Mr. Fanshawe. William Fanshawe had been an intimate friend of the Earl's; he was a witness to his will, and now (courteous as Rochester himself) he came to visit him. He was brought to the bedside, and there instead of weak, reminiscent profanities, he was met by an unexpected energy of attack. This penitent had become a propagandist—" Fanshawe, think of a God!" The visitor was reminded of the ill they had done together. " There is a good and a powerful God, and a terrible God." No John Wilmot but a Caroline John Baptist exhorted him. As soon as the Baptist closed exhausted eyes and mouth, Mr. Fanshawe, who had found nothing to say— it was no possible cue of his—fled. Before leaving the house he suggested that it would be a good thing if the Earl could be kept from such melancholy fancies. Having done his best, as he conceived, for the unfortunate invalid, he went off, and presently spoke somewhat disparagingly of his friend's mental state. When the news of it came to Woodstock the Dowager Countess lost Christian love in a rage. She wished that wretch Fanshawe had only as great a sense of sin—" he is an ungrateful man to such a friend." She told her son, unnecessarily, one would think, of Fanshawe's reports, and the Earl of Rochester— he was young in the new life—was moved. " I told my son," wrote the Dowager, " that I heard Mr. Fanshawe said that he hoped that he would recover, and leave those principles he now professed. He answer'd : ' Wretch ! I wish I had convers'd, all my lifetime, with link-boys, rather than with him and that crew ; such, I mean, as Fanshawe is. Indeed, I would not live, to return to what I was, for all the world.' " He was, no

THE WAY OF CONVERSION 257

doubt, truly repentant, but it was, according to his nature, a romantic repentance still.

Of one name he said nothing. One of his physicians, "thinking to please him," told him that Charles Stuart had lately drunk his health. John Wilmot looked fixedly at the doctor for some while, then, saying nothing, he turned his face away. It is not recorded that he uttered any pious hope for the King; the double nature which they had shared for so long, they shared to the end. There, rather than in any other mind, masculine or feminine, lay the intellectual understanding of John Wilmot; even to the day, five years later, when in Whitehall Father Huddleston came to offer his second service, and to aid the mortality of the King in his departure through his final twilight, as twenty-four years earlier he had companioned him in their night walk to meet Henry Wilmot. The silence of Henry Wilmot's son, prolonged as it were, through that turning away of his head, a recognition of something more than political loyalty in his father's phrase, "My master, your master, the master of us all."

He did his best to nullify Mr. Fanshawe's reports. He wrote a Declaration, countersigned by the Dowager and the Reverend Mr. Parsons, "for the benefit of all those whom I may have drawn into sin by my example and encouragement," in which he alluded to his former wicked life, pernicious opinions, and vile practices, confessed that he had lived without hope and without God in the world, and exhorted all his iniquitous friends to repentance. He wrote at more length, to the same effect, with even stronger adjectives about himself, his friends, and Almighty God, to Thomas Pierce, Dean of Salisbury. It must be admitted that these letters, if they are genuine, are depressingly below the brevity and directness of his usual style. Certainly, as he says at the beginning of the second, " my indisposition renders my intellectuals almost as feeble as my person." Alas! it is not the feebleness, it is not the flatness, that is so depressing. It is possible to hope that the Dowager and the clergymen composed the greater part of the letters; Rochester may have felt that his own verbal style was yet unequal to the proper technique of this miracle-play.

In July, Burnet came, and was with him for four days. Burnet was one of the best of all people to be with him, for Burnet was not one to make amendment too easy or repentance too theatrical. Rochester was always Rochester, and—admirably intelligent though he was—sometimes drama and sometimes lordship unintentionally got the better of him. Burnet was not a man to stand religious drama, he who thought the mystics " recluse melancholy people." Between the early seventeenth and early eighteenth centuries the steadfast Scot walked firmly on earth, with his eyes on his own rational heaven. The conversations of the winter were renewed in the high summer; George Fox lost a little ground. The ardent spirit of the Earl was dwelling on repentances. He saw them as suitable to the fifth act of the divine comedy. Burnet preferred them in the second or third; later, he said, they were commonly like " the howlings of condemned prisoners for pardon." " Little reason to encourage any to hope much from such sorrowings "; still, he admitted, they might—rarely—be effectual. He made it remarkably clear that the Earl, if he lived, must exhibit a wholly changed life, as evidence of that change of heart which was the only thing that mattered. The Earl, hoping for the best if he lived, said he thought on the whole that, if it pleased God, he would rather die; and added, with a sudden sweet ingenuousness, that he knew he could never again be in such health that life would be comfortable for him. It is possible to believe that Rochester could smile at his own dilemma; though he acted, he played a sincere part and could laugh at the difficulties of the technique. Sometimes he made a slip. One of his servants was slow in coming to him. Rochester said impatiently, "that damned fellow." Burnet took no notice at the time, but spoke of it later. The Earl (according to Burnet) answered : " Oh, that language of fiends which was so familiar to me, hangs yet about me ; sure none has deserved more to be damned than I have done." In an enthusiasm of penitence he asked Burnet to call the man, that he might beg his forgiveness also, but such *mots de théâtre* were too melodramatic for the more sober priest. "I told him that was needless, for he had said it of one that did not hear it, and so could not be offended by it." So the Earl was denied his incidental climax, or left to provide it interiorly for himself.

He was sincere enough. He gave orders that a *History of the Intrigues of the Court* which he had begun to write should be burned ; most unfortunately, he was obeyed. Similarly he destroyed "lewd songs." He returned again and again to Isaiah, causing his wife and his mother to read the Messianic chapter to him, and at last he had it by heart. "He made heavenly prayers " ; they also, less unfortunately, do not remain. But he remained in doubt— for the first time in his life—of his own capacity.

Could he play, for the rest of the run of his life, the part to which he had given his romantic and converted spirit? The monotony of the religious life is like every other monotony—only more so; the simplicity of sanctity lies far away. Until that simplicity is reached, and the actor is lost in the part, the *ceremonarius* in his office, there is bound to be division. Cues will be misunderstood; lines forgotten, gestures ineffective, and angelic silence instead of angelic applause will fill the universal theatre on the boards of which the postulant moves. Elizabeth Barry, for all of Lord Rochester's instructions, had made her début, and failed. Lord Rochester knew that he also might fail. Elizabeth Barry had returned and succeeded. Lord Rochester was haunted by a fear lest, if he failed, he should refuse to return, lest he should impatiently throw up his part in the plot of reconciliation and splendour, and escape from it to those other pitiful provincial pretences of Whitehall and the City. "What a wretch were I if I should fall away now!" He clung to Burnet, who played his own part so well, who knew his lines, who spoke them so mightily by the death-bed of Mrs. Roberts or by his own, and so carried on, unfaltering, the plot of the drama of all living, the drama of adoration and love.

But Burnet had indeed his own part to play, and that part bade him make his exit from Woodstock. He was compelled to return to London. Whoever or whatever so designed, designed also that Lord Rochester should be asked to do no more than practise this one romantic entry. It permitted him to escape, at any rate on the boards of this world, the bitter training of the company of the saints. It allowed him a little gesture of departure. Burnet had made an effort to leave on 23rd July, but the Earl desired him to stay that day "not without some passion." The doctors advised that a formal leave-taking would be undesirable. Consequently, at four in the morning of Saturday, 24th July 1680, Burnet quietly left the house. Presently one told my lord, who "seeming to be troubled" said: "Has my friend left me? Then I shall die shortly." He was allowed to do so. For "after that he spake but once or twice till he died: he lay much silent: once they heard him praying very devoutly. And on Monday about two o'clock in the morning he died, without any convulsion, or so much as a groan."

They buried him in a vault near the north aisle of Spilsbury Church, by the side of his father Henry. Eighteen months after, on 7th December 1681, they laid by him his young son Charles, a boy of ten. The direct line of his house was extinguished. "Another had his office"; in that very year King Charles bestowed the title of Rochester on that careful statesman Laurence Hyde—the son of that Hyde who had despised Henry Wilmot and kissed John Wilmot when he became Master of Arts at Oxford. Laurence, to complete the relation, was afterwards to prove himself a patron of Dryden, less exacting, less variable, less capacious than his predecessor. John Wilmot was left to sin and to repent, for two centuries, both in the most lurid colours, for the edification of the religious rabble whom the Earl of Rochester had magnificently despised. He had offered to be a link-boy, and after his death he became indeed a kind of fearsome link-boy, both to hell and heaven, for the right direction of the evangelical faithful.

CHAPTER XI

The Way of Union

The funeral sermon was preached by the Reverend Mr. Parsons; it was afterwards published by the request of the two Countesses. The text was St. Luke xv. 7—on the joy of the angels over the sinner that repenteth. The heavenly orchestra, under Mr. Parson's conducting, made music, in its usual rather ostentatious manner, over the return of John Wilmot, more and louder than it made over just persons, such as Dr. Burnet or Mr. Parsons himself. Just persons are a little hardly treated by the Gospels. On this occasion, however, it was at least understood that the penitent had enthusiastically invited the rejoicings. The Lord Rochester had made no suggestion that any of his wanderings had been the means of heavenly grace, nor that the light of celestial revelation had illumined any of his terrestrial loves. The dichotomy, in his mind, had been for the moment complete.

In the sermon Mr. Parsons, thinking of the fifty-third chapter of Isaiah, spoke again of that other dichotomy of which one term had so entirely triumphed over the other. He exclaimed in admiration at "the captivating all-humane imaginations to the obedience of a despised Religion and a crucified Saviour." He approved, if he did not entirely share, the enthusiasm of his penitent for the supreme romantic fact which so entirely satisfied the most extreme romantic desires. He added that my lord had intended, had he lived, to turn his wit, "instead of pitching upon a Beast or a Lust . . . to celebrate the mysteries of the Divine Love." "This was the vow and purpose of his sickness." Mr. Parsons contemplated with mingled sadness and resignation those Divine Poems which now the Lord Rochester, among choral saints and sweet societies, would never write.

Yet in fact, in the 1707 edition of Rochester's poems, twenty-seven years after the funeral oration, there appeared a poem which was said to be his, which was found not to be his, and yet may after all be his after another manner. It was a poem named only *To his Mistress*, and for more than two centuries its superb passion made it, for all who cared for that kind of thing, one of the great love poems of the language—a love poem of a very particular kind, a love poem in which love became religion, and all the phrases of religion were justly and with no profanation applied to the illumined passion of love. It was a theological ode in praise of romantic love; a hymn of that Romantic Theology which is the name of the divine science in its application to the equally divine experience. "To his Mistress"—

> Thou art my way; I wander if thou fly;
> Thou art my light; if hid, how blind am I;
> Thou art my life; if thou withdraw'st, I die.

It was attributed to Rochester, with what excuse we do not know. For the original was not Rochester's, but from that Jacobean poet Francis Quarles, who had died three years before Rochester was born. In his *Emblems, Divine and Moral*, published in 1635, the poem had first appeared as a devotional poem to Christ. "Why wilt thou shade that lovely face?" sang that intensity of adoring desire. In a mood of piety or profanity, or some like twisted intensity of both, another mind, which recognized the strength of the poem, changed it to another but related vision. Throughout it turned the vocatives from God and Lord to Love, ambiguously doubled for the god and the woman. Thereafter it was published as Rochester's; there is no reason why it should not be his. He certainly, of all those Restoration poets, was most capable of its genius.

In 1676 Sir George Etherege had published his comedy, *The Man of Mode*, of which the hero was a fine gentleman named Dorimant. "It was unanimously agreed that he had in him several of the Qualities of Wilmot, Earl of Rochester, as, his Wit, his Spirit, his amorous Temper, the Charms that he had for the fair Sex, his Falsehood, and his Inconstancy." Other characters in the play helped to define what the behaviour of Dorimant suggested. "Our journeyman, nowadays, instead of harmless ballads, sing nothing but your damn'd Lampoons," says a shoemaker. "You," cries out one of his disappointed mistresses, "who have more pleasure in the Ruin of a Woman's Reputation than in the endearments of her love!" And Dorimant himself confesses, "I never knew what 'twas to have a settled ague yet, but now and then have had irregular fits." It was the brilliant picture of a brilliant figure, the John Wilmot of the playhouse and the Court. Many of his hours were shown in it; one hour was not. The stress of his poetry was hardly there, nor the other twin stress of his spirit which answered to his poetry. The energy of his heart beat all ways; he mocked what he believed, and believed what he mocked. Into the rare union of those contending desires he hardly rose, nor was his age tolerant of such ascents. He hovered always towards it, the union of knowledge and wonder, intelligence and sensation, worship and laughter; towards joyous and sciential adoration. It was therefore that he, if indeed it were he, at some moment when either his profanity overmocked his piety or his piety overruled his profanity, and his passion and his poetry both, either in his wooing of Elizabeth Mallet, or in a half-serious teasing of Anne Temple, or in an interchange of genius with Elizabeth Barry, or with none of all these nor any other image of the flying moment, the greatness and not the fragility of which he so ardently desired, but in a sudden apprehension of that lovely tradition of Love in which body and spirit are truly one; in some such moment, turning the pages of *Divine Emblems*, he made as it were an emblem for himself, and rewrote devotion in the style which, forbidden mastery, he served in his heart. He cried to the lady of his moment, and to someone or something more than she. Let the poem stand as it was attributed to him, and not as Quarles wrote it :

> Why dost thou shade thy lovely face ? O why
> Does that eclipsing hand of thine deny
> The sunshine of the Sun's enliving eye ?

THE WAY OF UNION

Without thy light what light remains in me?
Thou art my life; my way, my light's in thee;
I live, I move, and by thy beams I see.

Thou art my life—if thou but turn away
My life's a thousand deaths. Thou art my way—
Without thee, Love, I travel not but stay.

My light thou art—Without thy glorious sight
My eyes are darken'd with eternal night.
My Love, thou art my way, my life, my light.

Thou art my way; I wander if thou fly.
Thou art my light; if hid, how blind am I!
Thou art my life; if thou withdraw'st, I die.

My eyes are dark and blind, I cannot see:
To whom or whither should my darkness flee,
But to that light? and who's that light but thee?

If I have lost my path, dear lover, say,
Shall I still wander in a doubtful way?
Love, shall a lamb of Israel's sheepfold stray?

My path is lost, my wandering steps do stray;
I cannot go, nor can I safely stay;
Whom should I seek but thee, my path, my way?

And yet thou turn'st thy face away and fly'st me!
And yet I sue for grace and thou deny'st me!
Speak, art thou angry, Love, or only try'st me?

Thou art the pilgrim's path, the blind Man's eye,
The dead Man's life. On thee my hopes rely:
If I but them remove, I surely die.

Dissolve thy sunbeams, close thy wings and stay!
See, see how I am blind, and dead, and stray!
. . . O thou that art my life, my light, my way!

Then work thy will! If passion bid me flee,
My Reason shall obey, my wings shall be
Stretch'd out no farther than from me to thee!

INDEX

Adderbury, 156, 163, 166–8.
Albemarle, Duke of, formerly General Monk, 15, 16, 54, 98.
Anne, Princess, 136, 138.
Aston, Colonel, 105–10.

Bagot, Miss, 57–8.
Balfour, Dr., 29, 30.
" Ballers," the, 173–4.
Barry, Elizabeth, 117–22, 157, 212–3, 225, 247, 252, 261, 268.
Belloc, Mr. Hilaire, 209.
" Bendo, Alexander," 191–9.
Bergen, Battle of, 44–8, 53.
Blagge, Margaret, 139.
Brouncker, Henry, 41–2, 199.
Buckhurst, Lord, 116, 141, 144, 153, 174, 179, 200, 210.
Burnet, Gilbert, 5, 11, 30, 264; and the Mystics, 6, 229; on " enthusiasm " and " extravagance," 6, 7, 94–5, 255; and Rochester, 22, 119, 172, 186–7, 219, 225–42, 247–8, 253, 258–262; reproves the Duke of York, 87–8; Charles II.'s dislike of, 226, 227; at the deathbed of Mrs. Roberts, 226–7, 261.
Butler, Lord John, 33, 39.
Butler, Mr., 207.

Castlemaine, Lady. See Villiers, Barbara.
Charles II., 19, 20, 32, 83–9, 100–4, 151, 257; flight after Worcester, 1–2, 9–10, 257; in France, 3, 11–5; and Lady Castlemaine, 16, 19, 34, 59, 85–6, 96, 97, 138; lands at Dover, 16–7, 23; love of the Bible, 17, 23; poems by Rochester to, 24–6, 96, 98–9, 132, 133, 167, 180–2, 243;

encourages Rochester's suit to Miss Mallet, 34–5, 39; sends Rochester to the Tower, 36–7; commends Rochester to Lord Sandwich, 42–3; bestows £750 on Rochester, 52; and Frances Jennings, 59; Rochester's epitaph on, 99; and Henry Savile, 114; and Settle, 132; adventure with Rochester, 176–175; a supper with Rochester, 200; and the Popish Plot, 215–7; and Mrs. Roberts, 226–7.
Chatham, Dutch at, 54 and *n*.
Cibber, Colley, 119.
Clifford, Lord, 53.
College, Stephen, 54 *n*., 163–5.
Cooke, Sarah, 57–8, 62, 64–5, 68–9, 71–2, 77, 78, 117–8, 247.
Cowley, admired by Rochester, 21, 25, 82–3.
Crowne, John, 133, 135–40, 143, 199, 214.

Davies, Moll, 86, 97, 138.
Dennis, John, 133.
Ditchley, 10, 13, 19.
Downs, Mr., 187–8.
Dryden, John, 100, 135, 137, 222, 228–9, 244, 263; Mulgrave his patron, 105, 131, 145, 151; and Rochester, 21, 123–34, 140, 143–4, 145–53, 166, 263; on Crowne, 140; on Oldham, 145; *Absalom and Achitophel*, 90, 116; *All for Love*, 146–9, 150 *n*.; *Astræa Redux*, 25–6; *Conquest of Granada*, 129; *Essay on Satire*, 153; *The Indian Emperor*, 38; *Marriage à la Mode*, 123–9.
Eliot, Mr. T. S., 175.
Epsom, 93, 179, 187.

Etherege, Sir George, 122, 128, 141, 172, 179, 187, 267.
Evelyn, John, 139.
Exclusion Bill, the, 216–7.

Fane, Sir Francis, 141.
Fanshawe, William, 255–6, 257.
Floyd, Mr., 208.
Foster, Miss, 206.
Fox, George, 2–5, 7–8, 9, 11, 18, 31, 32, 50, 52, 84, 92, 171, 216, 219, 251, 259.

Giffard, Rev. Francis, 21, 22, 223–5, 237.
Gwynn, Nell, 38, 91, 97, 101, 102, 190, 200, 217.

Hamilton, Anthony, his *Memoirs of the Count de Grammont*, 56, 57, 78 n., 79, 111, 117, 189–90, 199, 220, 221.
Hawley, Lord, 33, 35–6.
Hearne, Thomas, 21.
Herbert, Lord, 38–9.
Hinchingbrooke, Lord, 33–4, 37, 38, 39, 43.
Hobart, Miss, 57–78, 105.
Hobbes, Thomas, 8–9, 11, 16, 18, 65, 84, 158, 218, 225, 236.
Howard, Lady Elizabeth, 132–3.
Huxley, Mr. Aldous, 155.
Hyde, Anne, Duchess of York, 28, 57, 58, 62, 64, 77–8, 87.
Hyde, Edward, Earl of Clarendon, 14, 15, 28, 34, 57, 90, 263.
Hyde, Laurence, Earl of Rochester, 54, 263.

James, Duke of York, afterwards James II., 28, 35, 38, 41–2, 59, 84–9, 91, 114, 121, 122, 176, 199, 211, 216–7, 243.
Jennings, Frances, 58–60, 64, 199.
Jermyn, Henry, 86, 90.
Jones, Rice, 4–5, 9.
Joyce, Mr. James, 155.

Kerouaille, Louise de la, Duchess of Portsmouth, 97, 151, 152, 190, 200, 217–8, 243.
Killigrew, Sir Thomas, 13, 100–4.
Killigrew, Henry, 72–6, 78, 100, 103, 173, 190, 200.

Lee, Sir Henry, 19.
Lee, Henry, 22.
Lee, Nathaniel, 140, 143.
Lyttelton, Sir Charles, 66, 74, 75, 78.

Mallet, Elizabeth, afterwards Countess of Rochester, 56, 78 n., 85, 174, 268; and her mother-in-law, 19, 80, 157–160, 162 n., 165; her suitors, 33–4, 37, 38, 39, 43; abducted by Rochester, 35–6; marries Rochester, 39, 53; correspondence with Rochester, 39–40, 80, 156–62; at Woodstock, 154, 156; writes poetry, 162; a Roman Catholic, 163–5, 249; at Rochester's bedside, 247, 249, 253–4, 260; returns to the Protestant religion, 253, 255.
Mallet, John, 50–2.
Marvell, Andrew, 91–2.
Mary, Princess, 134–6, 138, 214.
Montagu, Edward, 45, 46–8.
Montagu, Sydney, 45.
Mulgrave, Lord. *See* Sheffield, John.

Newmarket, 177–8, 182, 184.

Oates, Titus, 215, 218, 242.
Oldham, John, 144–5.
Otway, Thomas, 121–2, 143.

Parsons, Rev. Robert, 249–50, 257, 264–5.
Pepys, 32, 34, 36, 37, 86, 101, 102, 138, 173 and n., 176, 210.
Plague, the, 35, 37–8, 189.
Pope, on Rochester, 113.
Popham, Sir Francis, 39.
Popish Plot, 16, 54 n., 91, 116, 134, 164, 215–9, 226, 229, 242.
Porter, James, 106–8.
Portsmouth, Duchess of. *See* Kerouaille, Louise de la.
Price, Goditha, 60, 68, 74, 199.

Quarles, Francis, 266, 268.

Revenge, the, 44–9, 221.
Roberts, Mrs., 226–7, 261.
Rochester, Earl of. *See* Wilmot.

INDEX 273

St. James's Fight, 53.
Sandwich, Earl of, 34, 35, 37, 38, 42, 43–5, 52.
Sandwich, Lady, 36–7, 43.
Savile, Henry, 114, 150–1, 150 n., 152, 166, 172, 174–5, 189, 200, 208–14, 217–8.
Sedley, Sir Charles, 116, 141, 144, 172, 174–5, 209–10.
Settle, Elkanah, 131–4, 143, 199.
Shadwell, Thomas, 133, 143, 149, 199.
Sheffield, John, Earl of Mulgrave, 104–114, 116, 129, 131–2, 145, 150–1, 200, 218, 243, 252.
Sodom, 244 n.
Spragge, Sir Edward, 53.
Stewart, Frances, 35, 39, 59, 85, 86.
Swift, 113.

Teddiman, Sir Thomas, 44, 47.
Temple, Anne, 58–78, 105, 129, 268.
Theatres : Dorset Garden, 121 ; Drury Lane, 38, 101, 102, 120, 199.
Tunbridge Wells, 38.

Verney, Sir Ralph, 19, 21, 22, 39, 94, 237, 253.
Villiers, Barbara, afterwards Lady Castlemaine and Duchess of Cleveland, 16, 19, 32, 34, 35, 58, 59, 85–6, 96–7, 138, 167, 252.
Villiers, George, Second Duke of Buckingham, 53, 90–2, 94, 116, 128, 152, 172, 179–84, 216, 220, 242, 243, 244 n., 252.

Wadham College, Oxford, 22–3, 28–9.
Waller, Edmund, on Rochester, 200–3.
Whitehall, Dr., 24–7, 29, 223–4.
Wilmot, Anne, Countess of Rochester, 10, 18–22, 39, 98, 237 ; and her daughter-in-law, 19, 80, 157–60, 162 n., 165 ; correspondence with Rochester, 42 ; at Rochester's bedside, 247, 249, 253–8, 260 ; and William Fanshawe, 255–6.

Wilmot, Elizabeth. See Mallet.
Wilmot, Henry, first Earl of Rochester, 18, 262–3 ; after Worcester, 1–2, 9–10, 26 ; in exile, 11–2, 19, 28, 34, 104 ; sent to Ratisbon, 12–4, 19 ; returns to London, 14 ; escapes to Flanders, 15 ; death, 15.
Wilmot, John, Earl of Rochester, 10–1 ; born, 18 ; horoscope, 20–1 ; early education, 21–2 ; at Oxford, 22–3, 24, 27–9 ; becomes Earl of Rochester, 24 ; the "mad earl," 21–2, 24, 32, 229, 254 ; and Charles II., 22, 89, 176–8, 257 ; poems to the King, 24–5, 96, 98–9, 132, 133, 167, 180–2, 243 ; receives degree from Clarendon, 28, 263 ; travels in Europe, 29–30 ; comes to Court, 31–3 ; abducts Elizabeth Mallet, 33–6 ; sails under Lord Sandwich, 38, 43 ; marries Elizabeth Mallet, 39, 53 ; on the *Revenge*, 44–8 ; agreement with Windham, 46–49, 185 ; mentioned in dispatches, 52 ; Gentleman of the Bedchamber, 52, 53, 180 ; bravery in the St. James's Fight, 53 ; and the Hobart-Temple affair, 57–79, 129, 268 ; and Sarah Cooke, 58, 62, 64–5, 68–9, 71–2, 77, 78, 117–8 ; verses on Goditha Price, 60, 68, 74 ; forbidden the Court, 78, 98, 103, 178, 182, 189 ; letters to Lady Rochester, 39–40, 80, 156–62 ; lampoon on the Duke of York's conversion, 88–9 ; and Lady Castlemaine, 32, 34, 96–7, 167, 252 ; strikes Sir Thomas Killigrew, 102–3 ; on poetry, 95, 104, 186, 221, 250 ; quarrel with Lord Mulgrave, 104–114, 145, 150–1, 243 ; in Paris, 103 ; quarrel with Lord Dunbar, 114 n. ; and Elizabeth Barry, 117–122, 157, 212–3, 225, 252, 261, 268 ; patron of Otway, 121–2, 143 ; patron of Dryden, 123–8, 263 ; separation from Dryden, 128–33, 140, 143, 166 ; patron of Settle, 131–4, 143 ; patron

of Crowne, 135–40, 143; Sir Francis Fane on, 141; patron of Lee, 141, 143; attack on Dryden, 21, 145–53; and Oldham, 144; letters to Saville, 150–1, 150 n., 152, 208–14, 217–8; his children, 159, 162, 174, 212–3, 263; tales of his disguises, 167–8, 188–99; his private sentry, 170–2; and the "Ballers," 173–4; sensational adventures, 176–205; destruction of the dial, 179; and the death of Mr. Downs, 187–8; as "Alexander Bendo," 191–9; illnesses, 161, 166, 206, 212, 214, 247–262; and Miss Foster, 207–8; alleged nudity, 210–1; elected Alderman for Taunton, 214; speaks against the Exclusion Bill, 216; and Burnet, 225–242, 247–8, 253, 258–62; and the Rev. R. Parsons, 249–50, 257; conversion, 250–62, 264–265; death and burial, 262–3; funeral sermon on, 264–5.

All my Past Life, 142; *An Allusion to Horace*, 146; *The Commons' Petition to King Charles II.*, 181–2; *History of the Intrigues of the Court*, 260; *The Imperfect Enjoyment*, 18, 203; *To a Lady that accused him of Inconstancy*, 172; *Lais Senior*, 97; *The Maim'd Debauchee*, 204; *To his Mistress*, 265–6, 268–70; *Monster All-Pride*, 111; *Upon Nothing*, 142; *A Pastoral Courtship*, 155; *Prologue to the "Empress of Morocco,"* 132–3; *The Restauration, or the History of Insipids*, 180–1; *Rochester's Farewell, 1680*, 243; *The Royal Angler*, 133; *Sodom*, 244 n.; *Valentinian*, 244–7.

Windham, John, 45, 46–9.
Wood, Anthony, 95, 223–4, 244 n.
Woodstock, 150, 152, 154, 156, 166, 172–3, 174, 199, 210–1, 214, 247, 256, 262.
Wycherley, William, 149, 199.

www.ingramcontent.com/pod-product-compliance
Lightning Source LLC
Chambersburg PA
CBHW021145160426
43194CB00007B/694